W9-AQD-965

Morality and Expediency

THE LEWIS HENRY MORGAN LECTURES / 1975

The University of Rochester

Rochester, New York

Morality and Expediency

The Folklore of Academic Politics

F. G. Bailey

University of California
San Diego

WITH A FOREWORD BY ALFRED HARRIS

ALDINE PUBLISHING COMPANY · CHICAGO

First published in 1977 by Aldine Publishing Co.

Address all inquiries to:

Aldine Publishing Company
529 South Wabash Ave.
Chicago, Illinois 60605

ISBN 0-202-01159-3

Library of Congress Catalogue Number 77-78109

Printed in Great Britain

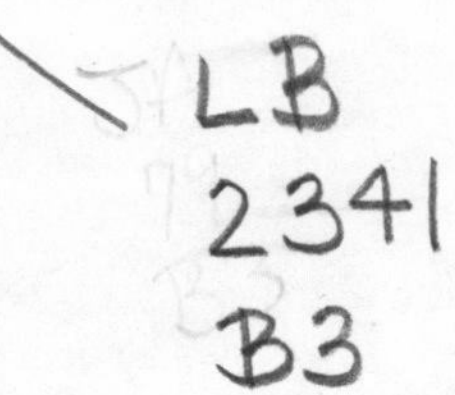

Contents

Foreword

In this much expanded version of his Lewis Henry Morgan Lectures, Professor Bailey carries on the tradition established by previous Lecturers. Since 1963,[1] successive lecturers have not only commemorated Morgan and his work; they have synthesized and explored various aspects of present-day anthropology, ordinarily in light of their own field data.

This particular volume presents in considerable detail Professor Bailey's exploration of American academic politics, and in it he develops his own approach to politics still further. Another volume from Professor Bailey's pen is to be welcomed, and it is worth stressing this one's special merits. As an anthropological study of academic politics in the United States it is an important contribution to a regrettably small body of professionally oriented work dealing with that area of political life. It will be more readily built upon than *Lucky Jim, The Masters* or *The Groves of Academe*. What makes this volume even more noteworthy, however, is the fact that it is by a highly qualified non-native who has nearly perfect comprehension of the (American) language. There are too few such studies, welcome though they are. This one will, of course, raise hackles or evoke vigorous assent. However, its capacity to provide strong stimulus for additional work on the subject is of special importance, and Professor Bailey offers this stimulus in full measure.

Professor Bailey's Lectures were delivered to appreciative audiences on September 30 to October 9, 1975. Absence on leave prevented me from enjoying them, though those who heard him, and attended his seminars, have commented at length on Professor Bailey's readiness to discuss and debate —and even, on occasion, to compromise.

Alfred Harris, Editor
Lewis Henry Morgan Lectures

[1] The connection of Lewis Henry Morgan with the University of Rochester, and the initiation of the Morgan Lectures in 1963, are briefly discussed in the Foreword to Professor Meyer Fortes' *Kinship and the Social Order* (Aldine, 1960).

Introduction

In a sentence which breathes the sobriety of his times Morgan wrote: 'There is enough, within the limits of the veritable, which is sufficiently remarkable, without entering the domain of fancy to produce a picture' (1868, p. 35). The judgement—about the American beaver—seems apt enough to one who reads his book on that ingenious animal, but it also gives rise to the thought that for all the imagination that seems to have gone into *Ancient Society,* Morgan himself never knowingly entered the 'domain of fancy' and would have disdained, in his scientific endeavours, to do so. As a naturalist, he allowed no place for myth.

As a student of society, he was no less straightforward. One senses the approval with which he wrote the following: 'Dissimulation was not an Indian habit. In fact, the language of the Iroquois does not admit of double speaking, or of the perversion of the words of the speaker. It is simple and direct, not admitting those shades of meaning and those nice discriminations which pertain to polished languages' (1962, p. 334). With all respect to the shade of Morgan, and with no knowledge whatsoever of the Iroquois language, that is very hard to swallow. The Iroquois of those times are known for their singularly successful political confederation. How does one run any political enterprise in a language that does not admit of dissimulation?

In his other life—as a lawyer and a politician—Morgan no doubt made the acquaintance of fancy and pretence and dissimulation and even fraud, and his biographers, Resek and Stern, both show him marginally involved in the egregious scandals of his time and place, not, certainly as a protagonist, but not, either, in a role where innocent unawareness could have been a possibility. 'The channels are devious.' he wrote 'It takes a politician to row the boat, which I am not' (*Resek,* p. 119). But Resek, the biographer, writing of an ingenious swindle perpetrated by Morgan's associates in the Erie Railroad, tells us, 'For all the appearances that he gave us of an abstracted scholar, Morgan was an eminently practical man. In the absence of an efficient railroad regulation, the maintenance of competition was the only guarantee of reasonable shipping prices. For the time being, defense of the Erie's methods seemed a necessary if unwholesome solution' (*Resek* p. 118).

This book commemorates that side of mankind's activities which Morgan pretended and every public figure pretends does not exist. It is about institutionalized facades, make-believe and pretence, lies and hypocrisy, and other such performances. Of men Morgan writes, '. . . their progress has been found to be in exact proportion to the wisdom of the institutions under which their minds were developed' (1962, p. 57). In this book I make two arguments that would have drawn expressions of shock from the public *persona* of Morgan: our survival—forget about progress—depends upon a collective act of make-believe, a venture into the domain of fancy where we can assure ourselves that the world and men are basically orderly and predictable; and, secondly, that our institutions must so develop our minds that we can become 'eminently practical' men in the interests of solving our problems by finding the least objectionable solution, whatever damage it might do to our principles.

Morgan the scholar and Morgan the moralist would certainly have bridled: Morgan the man of affairs must have lived in this practical unprincipled way.

It is singularly difficult to penetrate to the unprincipled side, when working in a political culture other than one's own. Not only do people have a proper reticence about letting a stranger, no matter how well-disposed, behind the scenes, but also the back stage of politics is played out in a language of great subtlety which is often beyond the reach of those who are not native speakers. Admittedly, one loses something of the fresh perceptive eye when looking at the familiar, but in this instance I thought the price worth paying and the 'natives' in this ethnography are my colleagues.

But there is a danger. If I list those who have assisted me with comment and criticism—the members of my department, some elder statesmen on this campus, Robert Elliott, Roy Harvey Pearce, Paul Saltman and Avrum Stroll, and my colleagues in travail, Tom Dunseath and Robert Erickson—it may be thought that this is no more than a fragmentary history of the La Jolla Campus, or at best a *livre à clef*. It is nothing of the sort. Firstly the catchement of my own experience and of others' information is much wider: Phil Gulliver, Ken Burridge, Abner Cohen, Jeremy Boissevain, James Peacock and his colleagues in North Carolina, and one who knows the scene much more deeply than I do, Harry L. Levy. Secondly, this is not a history: it is an effort at generalization, an attempt to explore themes and procedures and to ask questions about universities anywhere and organizations anywhere.

Four of the chapters in this book were delivered as the Morgan Lectures at the University of Rochester in the autumn of 1975 and to my friends there I owe an especial debt: to Al Harris for making the invitation; to Walter Sangree for his gentle and considerate hospitality; to graduate students and faculty, especially Fitz John Poole for pertinent and constructive criticism and for their kind hospitality.

The staff of my department has been unfailingly helpful. Mary Petrovits smoothed the way and the long task of typing and re-typing was efficiently done by Marcia Bradley and Kathy Clark.

I dedicate this book to the memory of Gerald E. Williams who died before his time.

Del Mar
California
1 June 1976

F. G. Bailey

CHAPTER ONE

Myth, Reality, and Politics

Three Callings

Invoking the name of Lewis Henry Morgan, we honor a scholar industrious in the collection of fact and ingenious in its interpretation; a man of collegial bent, rejoicing in the company and the conversation of others who, like Morgan himself, took their pleasures in serious discussion of the serious intellectual questions of their day; thirdly we honor a man who was deeply involved in the world, as a lawyer, as a man with investments to manage and—from time to time and without great success—as a candidate for and holder of political office.[1] Those three aspects of Morgan's life represent the 'academic dilemma'. In fact we should call it a 'trilemma', since there are three horns on which to lose one's academic manhood.

Firstly Morgan was interested in answering intellectual questions: in collecting facts, discovering a pattern within them, and solving problems as yet unsolved. For him, as for any scholar, this activity was, in some degree at least, an end in itself. He was unstinting in the time and energy and expense which he devoted to the understanding of kinship systems and the evolution of human societies. Of course, like anyone else, he rejoiced in fame and recognition, was hurt and annoyed by what seemed to him to be destructive criticism, but in no way can one imagine that 'fame was the spur'. For any scholar one part of his life is a contest between himself as an intellect and the brute disorderly objective universe of Nature. *The real satisfaction comes from perceiving a pattern where none was known before.* Whether or not the pattern will help people survive an illness or get more to eat or be slightly less objectionable to their fellows is an entirely secondary consideration. Knowledge, new knowledge, the satisfaction of intellectual curiosity is its own reward.

The second horn is collegiality, membership of the community of learning. Morgan, like some but not all scholars, enjoyed the community of his fellows and was an enthusiastic organizer and joiner of learned societies, the object of which was the exchange of information and opinions on scholarly topics. These societies and the correspondence in which he engaged increasingly as his reputation grew, constituted for him the equivalent of his 'university', his 'community of learning' (what was missing was the urge to teach the young: he refused an invitation to join Cornell, saying that he had neither the patience nor the temperament to undertake such work). At first sight membership of the community of scholars is no more than an extension of private enquiry and entirely complementary to it; from exchange and criticism come new ideas; and, indeed, it is a truism that knowledge which is not disseminated and made available for scrutiny by others is not knowledge at all. In fact the matter is not so simple and, to an important extent, some forms of interaction with other scholars tend to blunt the fine point of scholarly inquiry or at least to restrict the range of its probing.

Morgan's third life, and the third horn of the 'trilemma' was the world beyond scholarship. For Morgan, as for the rest of us, there was a reciprocity in this third aspect of his life. As a successful lawyer, man of business, and an indifferently successful politician, he made the living which provided resources for his scholarship. We too depend on resources got from outside to maintain our scholarly activities, but in a way different from that of Morgan: for us the subsidy is direct, and is available to the extent that the world outside can be convinced that what goes on in universities is worthwhile. The other direction is the obligation, felt strongly by Morgan and to a very varying extent by scholars of the present day, to provide the kind of knowledge which will make life better in the world beyond the Academy. Morgan, as you well know, was a lifetime champion of Indian causes and, more generally, held the conviction common in his day, that knowledge was for use and that reason was the path to follow in perfecting society.

There is a fourth aspect to life in universities which, since three horns are enough, can be regarded as a branch of the third: involvement with the world of power and resources. This road, within a university, is trodden by service on committees and by accession to positions of power as a departmental chairman or an academic administrator. These people (together with those who stay away from such responsibilities) will be the principal actors in my play. These are the people who, to pick up one of Morgan's concerns, must never be allowed to exercise power in an arbitrary fashion. But they are also the gatekeepers, extracting resources from the world outside, adapting standards of scholarship to meet the realities of that world and keeping out the forces of evil and disruption.

Summarizing, there are three kinds of goals:[2] the pursuit of learning for its own sake; the benefit to be derived from belonging to a community; and the goal of power. These goals may occasionally complement one another, but mainly they contradict.

Given three or more captains on the bridge, none agreed upon a destination and none strong enough to eliminate the others, if the ship is to move at all, one would expect procedures for reaching compromise. In order to examine these procedures we move first to discourse, which will be comfortingly familiar to an anthropologist or sociologist, but to those in other disciplines may seem frivolous, certainly unscientific and even threatening because it is subversive of all that a university stands for: the rule of reason and the existence of an objective truth. This discourse concerns myths.

Myths

A myth tells what one should desire (like scholarship, collegiality, or power) and how to get it; the way people are and how they should be; the reasons why things happen the way they do, especially when they go wrong; in short, myths provide values and meaning and ideas and plans and stratagems and alternative forms of social organization. Only through a myth does one see the 'real' world. A myth is a form of pretence, an oversimplified representation of a more complex reality.

You may wonder why the word 'myth' is used rather than such honored equivalents as 'collective representation', 'culture', 'values', 'ideas', 'plans', 'stratagems', 'personal constructs', 'eidos', 'ethos', 'cognitive map', 'value orientation', 'model', and so on. There is indeed a rich harvest of near-synonyms, but 'myth' suits my purpose best. Firstly, the Greek word from which it is derived has the primary meaning of the *spoken* word, and you will see later that an interest in face-to-face politics leads to a compelling curiosity about that which is not or cannot be codified, with communications which pass from the mouth to the ear, which frequently are kept behind the scenes, because they will cause embarrassment or they will self-destruct if they are subjected to codification and made open to everyone. This is an arena where finesse is king and the term 'myth', reminding us that the spoken word generally leaves open more options than the written rule, conveniently recalls that arena.

Secondly, 'myth' is attractive because the word has a nice mixture of the sacred and the derisory. In its second meaning in the Greek 'myth' means a fable, something which obviously is not true. When we say of another person's cherished beliefs that they are nothing more than 'myths' we mean firstly that they are fanciful and, secondly, that the other person, because he believes in them, has to be either stupid or cynical (only pretending belief for some ulterior motive). The suggestion that the other person is foolish or insincere can clearly be a move in a competition to gain power over him or to deny him power.

Anthropologists, in the same rubber-glove way that they handle terms like 'corruption' or 'faction', have tended to overlook this sense of purposeful derision and to ask instead what is the function of a myth and to imagine what would happen if those who believed were overnight turned into unbelievers. They ask sensible questions. To phrase anything in terms of function and dysfunction may tend to take the poetry out of it: but in this case, it should be remembered that the word 'myth' in the sense of a belief or a story or a value or a person somehow removed beyond the limits of doubt and questioning, accepted on faith alone, is the entire subject matter of religion. This is what the character Relling, in *The Wild Duck* called the 'Basic Lie that makes life possible'. The 'basic lies', how they fit or fail to fit one another, who holds them, what plans of action he derives from them, and what use he can make of them to manipulate other people, and, finally, what relation these lies bear to their complement ('reality' or 'experience') are the subject of this book. Politcs is the art of bringing unacceptable myths into, and preserving one's own myths from derision.

To summarize in a metaphor. Somewhere beyond us, 'out there', is a reality which is invisible, intangible, incomprehensible, inaccessible at least in any direct way. Nevertheless, although we have no *direct* apprehension of reality, like a person whose sight or hearing is defective, we can put on spectacles or use hearing aids and so begin to sense and feel and experience. But this sensing apparatus comes in many different styles and depending upon which type you happen to own or happen to choose, or happen to have thrust upon you, the world and people seem a different place. How some sets of apparatus are judged better than others in the light of experience is a problem to which we will come later. Meantime the metaphor is being used to make two summary points. Firstly, if the apparatus is destroyed, nothing is left, at least nothing that we can talk about. If you command me to cease talking about myths and mythical characters and to concentrate upon the 'reality' of university life, then either I must be silent or take this as an invitation to try out another set of myths to see if you can understand them better. That is the second summary point: you can visualize the politics of a university, or indeed any politics as an attempt to convince the other man that he would be better off if he used your spectacles instead of his own, either because they are better or because, if he persists in his refusal, you will beat in his head.[3]

Private and Public

The suggestion that a crack on the skull is the way to deal with someone who refuses to accept your myths about the way the world is and should be, brings us back to the subject of compromise.

When debate turns into argument and argument moves to quarrel, the contestants are backing away from the shared ground of reason and stockading themselves in principles. No longer does each expect to convince the other, still less to be himself won over, but both have become intent on asserting a truth which they believe but do not know how to demonstrate to someone who does not accept that truth as self-evident. Within the same society, within the same community, even within an organization principles stand in contradiction with one another often enough to make an orderly continuation of social life impossible, were it not for certain remedial devices.

One of these devices is a retreat from reason (reason requires a successful search for those common principles which would make debate possible) into ritual and ceremonial activity (which is the assertion of some general overriding all-transcending myth of commonality between the contestants: they are the children of the one God, dependent for their prosperity and health on his will, required to show harmony and mutual concern in his presence—or something of that nature.) Asserting this mutual dependency through symbolic activities, they apparently transcend irreconcilable differences of principle. But the differences remain unreconciled, the quarrels unresolved, and stand ready to break out again at some later time. Ritual, which appears to bring peace, in fact brings only a truce, doing nothing to change the conditions which at first allowed the debate to grow into a quarrel.

There is another way in which differences of principle can be resolved. It is done by enticing the contestants out of their principled stockades back into the field of reason and compromise and bargaining, where they discover that fundamental principles are not so fundamental after all and can be traded off against one another. When there is a trade-off—and there is, constantly—this process is pragmatic and practical. (It is also scientific to the extent that it deals with 'can' rather than 'should'.) It comes into operation when men stop trying to reason their way towards truth and become 'reasonable'.

To be 'reasonable' in this sense indicates that one is willing to abandon, or at least to compromise, a principle which one has publicly proclaimed to be fundamental, firm and unchanging—an eternal verity, sacred enough to defy negotiated erosion. The negotiations, accordingly, are likely to be conducted behind a screen of privacy. Our analysis comes to be dominated by the distinction between what is said out in the open, where anyone can listen, and what must be communicated to a more restricted audience. In the refusal to say what one thinks so that everyone can hear, in the often painfully learned hypocrisy of saving face and using the white lie, in the world of bluff and the hidden agenda and confidentiality and even gossip lie the mechanisms which preserve the purity and sanity-giving quality of principles which are asserted to be fundamental and unchangeable.

The procedures through which political contests are moved to and fro between the front and the back, not only prevent contests from degenerating into fights but also serve as a means of adjusting myths or principles or fundamental values to changing situations. Principles have consequences inasmuch as they are guides for action. Not all principles are fundamental. Some are offered as means to other desirable ends, and if these ends are not achieved, the principle is likely to be modified. But even those principles which are ends in themselves, nevertheless exist in a world of experience which may change so as to make their attainment impossible. While every normal person might accept that this side of heaven his ideals cannot be totally fulfilled, there is also a threshold of failure beneath which the ideal becomes pointless and is abandoned. In short, in looking at contradictory values and the trade-offs made between them, we are also looking at an adaptive system by which the whole corpus of values and 'eternal' verities finds adjustment with the world of experience.

So far we have two main distinctions: myth opposes reality or experience; political procedures are relatively public or relatively private. A third dimension links these two. The further it is removed from reality and experience, the more a myth takes on the style of caricature, a simplified bold outline of one, or at most a few, features.

This is also characteristic of open politics. Roughly speaking, the bigger the audience, the simpler the message. The reason is obvious: those who are engaged in politics, especially in open politics, are not looking for an objective truth: rather they are attempting to make a point of view stick, probably in the heat of the moment, probably before an audience which they sense is similarly combative, and in such conditions unqalified assertions of irrefutable truth, delivered with simplicity and directness, are more likely to win the day than a delicately sculptured, minutely reasoned and cautiously qualified, infinitely sophisticated exposition of a limited, but possibly tenable, point of view.

The range of myths, therefore, which occur in any particular kind of institution, is likely to be limited. University myths,[4] especially the competing themes of 'community' and 'organization' are the subject of the first part of the book (Chapters 2 and 3). Those who subscribe to the myth of organization look for a product, prefer one that can be measured and so insist on accountability, and define the normal and healthy relationship between people as essentially impersonal. The myth of community reverses each of these values: people are to be treated in the round, as ends in themselves rather than instruments at the service of an organization; the community has no particular product and is intrinsically valued, as an end in itself, and to ask for accountability is at best a misunderstanding and at worst a wicked perversion of the true nature of the institution. These and other myths contain values which both guide and are resources for actors, in their efforts to impose definitions of what is and what should be upon each other and upon an audience. We examine their use both within the university and in its interactions with the world outside.

The second part of the book (Chapters 4 and 5) examines arenas: sets of rules which lay down how competition should be conducted, and, beyond these, other 'rules' which advise not on how to play the game, but how to win.

The arenas vary between the poles of public and private. When the contest moves to a more private arena, the myths are brought nearer to reality, and people are less willing to comfort themselves with pretence because they can perceive more readily in a specific than in a general and abstract version of a myth the costs (or the benefits) of acting as if that myth were true. The myths of the back arena are still myths:

but more complicated, more technical, and less accessible to those actors who are long on heart and short on head.

The third section of the book (Chapters 6 and 7) describes the actors who appear on political stages and the masks which they wear (in universities and probably in other organizations, too). The range is limited (as with myths and for the same reasons). Abstraction and simplification, the tools of analysis, are also the tools of politics. As the writer communicates with his readers, so also does the politician both with opponents and supporters. Successful communication requires an ability to select and highlight some features, and leave others in the shade or obscured entirely. The actor has to know which mask to wear. Failure to match the selection to the audience makes an antagonist ineffectual; audiences come equipped with capacities and expectations and to make a presentation in a manner which is wholly unfamiliar, invites defeat. But—and in this lies one of the many paradoxes of politics—the unexpected act catches attention, disturbs the opponent, and properly used can bring victory.

To the extent that a particular contest is withdrawn from the public arena in the direction of privacy and compromise, so the messages can become more subtle and more complex. The actors show themselves willing to lose 'face' both in the sense that they are less concerned with their honor and in that they now exhibit a more rounded, more complex, more subtle and apparently less superficial version of themselves.

A Sermon

Do not look in this book for a solution to the 'real' problems which face universities.[5] Anthropologists seldom have the hubris to make recommendations, and in any case, if my argument is correct, the phrase 'real problem' is misleading because problems are what people choose to recognize as, or to persuade one another are, problems.

Problems go in and out of fashion. At one time students are rebellious and alienated; at another time they want facts and are contemptuous of ideas and ideals. The gateway to higher education is impossibly narrow and leaves much talent wasted in the wilderness beyond: the gates are so wide that classrooms are crowded out with poorly motivated, poorly trained and possibly untrainable students. There are many worries about resources, a sense of deprivation and gloom after some years of plenty, salaries limping along behind a galloping inflation, universities facing bankruptcy. There are also more parochial sources of distress: incompetent teachers; authoritarian insensitive administrators; colleagues who manage to exploit the system, leaving others to carry the burdens; and so forth.

If one grants these and similar problems the accolade of being 'real' in the sense that they are immediate and urgent, forcing people to work for a solution, one should not think that the other kind of problem is 'unreal'. That other kind of problem, which is the focus of this book, has no solution, but it is not trivial. For example, there is nothing insubstantial about the conflict between the demands of scholarship, collegial responsibilities and the obligations to a wider society: that three-way pull is the force in many of our immediate difficulties. But whereas there are ways of dealing with the incompetent colleague or the bullying administrator, there is no way of ending once and for all the conflict between one's obligations to a colleague and one's obligations to the discipline or the institution. In such cases, to look for the solution and the cure, to plan conclusively to resolve the dilemma, is to manipulate symbols—to reassure oneself, perhaps—rather than to act instrumentally upon a real world. A more sensible posture is that of the person who seeks instead to understand the nature of the inevitable, with the hope at best of alleviating symptoms and lessening discomfort. When dealing with problems of this high order, the services needed are those of the pathologist, rather than the physician.

Those anthropologists who affect the humility of a scientific attitude, would reject even the small element of moral judgement contained in the metaphor of the pathologist; denying that it is their business to advise on how health should be distinguished from sickness. Of course they do it all the time, and a major diversion is to open the door of a rival's intellectual closet and let the bones of his prejudice fall out. I open mine now and this will be the extent of my moralizing: most of the dangers are to be found on the front stage and among men of principle, the true believers; civilized people admit their doubts, exhibit some willingness to compromise and allow that other versions of 'better' may be as good as their own, and believe that nothing is so sacred that at least some of it cannot be given away. Apart from that, the book is about the way people behave (that is, the masks they wear and the myths they invoke), and how they understand what they are doing; not about the way they *should* behave and how to make them do so.

NOTES

1. Statements about Morgan's career and about his opinions are taken either from his own writings, or from two short biographies by C. Resek and B. J. Stern.

2. There are, of course, other goals besides the three or four which I have built into the analysis, most of them overlapping with one another. There is a neat and brief description of another trio—German intellectualism, American populism and the traditions of Victorian Oxford (stiffening the young with rectitude, a sense of duty, and some learning)—in *Kerr* (p. 48). My purpose however, is not to survey the many themes which are voiced today in Universities: nor is it to trace their antecedents and connections. Rather my interest is at a higher level of abstraction: in the fact that any organization or community will have values and standards which cannot all be reconciled with one another: and in the question of how

people deal with the problems which arise from such contradictions.

3. The meaning which I wish to impart to the word 'myth' does not depart substantially from common usages in anthropology and political science. 'Myth fulfils in primitive culture an indispensable function: it expresses, enhances, and codifies belief; it safeguards and enforces morality; it vouches for the efficiency of ritual and contains the practical rules for the guidance of man' (*Malinowski,* p. 79). There is nothing wrong with this statement for someone interested in politics, except the functionalist aroma of a well-ordered and tranquil world. A statement in *Sorel,* at the other extreme is equally acceptable. '. . . men who are participating in a great social movement always picture their coming action as a battle in which their cause is certain to triumph. These constructions . . . I propose to call myths; the syndicalist "general strike" and Marx's catastrophic revolution are such myths' (pp. 41-2). There follows an interesting discussion (pp. 41-6) in which Sorel (writing to Daniel Halevy) laments the way in which his readers have misunderstood his use of the word myth. Note particularly his scorn for those critics who miss the point and try to invalidate a myth by demonstrating that it lacks 'practical possibility'.

If one matches the commonplace everyday pervasive quality suggested in the quotation from Malinowski with the political significance of Sorel's usage, it can be seen that myths are not confined to 'great social movements' but are a feature of everyday political life.

As for the *credo quia absurdum* element, the high mysteries and the divine forces (see chapter 7 in *Cassirer*), certainly that aspect is important because it provides that inertia in social procedures which both helps because it gives us the illusion that we are in control of a stable world and hurts because it prevents us from responding readily to a changing environment. But there too (as in the case of Sorel's 'great social movements') one should notice that *credo quia absurdum* is used as a guide not only in the context of deep mysteries and divine forces but also in the petty struggles of everyday life.

4. We have a long tradition in anthropology of concealing a void of ideas behind a screen of exotic and bizarre fact, helped out by an appropriate selection of photographs. The material used to make the argument in this book is not exotic. Many of my readers will see the facts presented about tenure problems or the chairman caught between the anvil of the administration and the hammer of his colleagues, as life revisited: even the anecdotes are sometimes part of a familiar folklore—since writing chapter 2 I have found tales of other chairmen who forgot to submit the departmental budget. Consequently the superficial reader, one without the capacity or with a disdain for theory, finding no *exotica,* will conclude that he knows it all already. He skims the surface, feeding on the 'facts', and leaving untouched the ideas for which the facts are no more than a convenient vehicle, and issues his verdict: 'banal'. But the problems of pattern and connection and sequence in face-to-face politics are more efficiently examined when the mind is not distracted by the bizarre. If the facts are banal theory will better flourish.

5. Literature on universities—it is abundant—falls into three categories. There are serious studies by sociologists and social psychologists, including a great deal of self-study issued in the form of reports and plans, which for the most part I did not find useful. Much of it is would-be applied 'in-house' stuff, and especially that done by the cost-benefit gang, rendered less useful for my purpose because the determination to quantify caused political questions and issues to be somehow simplified out of the discussion. Also much of it is weakened by the bland assumption that all problems can be made to yield to reasoned solutions. Every university has its own stock of such literature. A heavyweight generalized example would be the book by *Parsons* and *Platt.* I would exempt from these strictures, although they fall into this category, works cited

under *Lunsford* and *Clark*.

The second category is both easier to read and for my purpose more productive. These are books by academics, often those who have made names for themselves as Presidents of Universities or Masters of Colleges. Being usually more than a little autobiographical, they are not entirely reliable as sources of fact, but they are splendid sources both of opinion about the eternal verities of university life and of practical advice about how to stay elegantly afloat, and even make headway, in the rough seas of academic controversy. *Kerr* is recommended as a starter.

The third category contains three sub-sections, each of which seems to have the very good and the unspeakable and little in between. One section is fiction: for those of the appropriate age and cultural background, there is nothing to beat *Lucky Jim* by Kingsley Amis. The second section, non-fictional but moralistic in the same direction, is well represented by Veblen's *The Higher Learning in America*. The final section has been spawned by the fame and fortune of *Parkinson's Law*. The format, apparently so easy, has produced a number of books by scholars, transparently in the grip of menopausal depression, so without fun or wit, so extravagant in their bitterness that they go far beyond satire and arouse only commiseration in the reader for an author whose life has turned so sour. In fact I have found nothing in this category which comes even near to that work of indisputable genius, first published in 1908 by F. M. Cornford, *Microcosmographia Academica*.

CHAPTER TWO

Community and Organization

Two Stories

Conversing about universities with a friend, I heard two stories and at first sight his values seemed the wrong way round: he was furiously indignant about a trifling matter, while amused and tolerant over the grossest negligence. Here are the stories.

A member of a social science department had proposed himself for advancement to a senior rank. At that university all advancements were considered by a scholar's peers, and on this occasion they unanimously and strongly advised the Dean that the advancement should *not* be made. The man had never written a book on his subject nor even contributed an article to a learned journal. But he did enjoy a wide reputation because he wrote newspaper commentaries on matters of public concern and gave a weekly program on local radio and television. He made his discipline and his university visible and audible and his file was filled with letters of recommendation from editors and politicians and other leading citizens. But no scholar, neither in his own university nor elsewhere, was willing to give him the testimonial appropriate to the high rank to which he aspired.

My friend had no doubts about the correct decision: deny the advancement. What the man did amounted at best to public relations and was in no sense a contribution to scholarship: in fact he was nothing more than—the word was an explosion of contempt—a 'popularizer'.

His other story was about a large department in which

several sub-disciplines were gathered, but hardly united, under one administrative cover. The chairman of this department had a difficult and thankless task, so much so that one particular chairman had given up any attempt to coordinate the subdisciplines, leaving them to manage their own internal affairs and to scheme against one another. He stayed away from his office, he stayed away from meetings, and he withdrew into the woodwork of his own scholarly concerns. When the academic year ended all forty or so members of the department dispersed to get on with their own work and came back in the Autumn to discover that the chairman had neglected to submit a budget, so that for the coming year this huge department was without funds. The structure of financing made it impossible to set the error right at once, and all kinds of ingenious recourse was had to various 'launderable' monies to pay for paper and typists and paper clips and secretaries and all the other academic consumables.

I am not sure that I believe this story. There are many funny ways to run a railroad, but none quite like that. The point, however, is not the truth of the story, but the fact that it was told, that it is part of a large corpus of tall stories about academic incompetence, which are related, as this one was, with great relish, with amusement, and with a total indulgence, even a touch of vicarious pride in the fact that academics can be so entirely cack-handed in business affairs.

My friend is a scholar and that is the way he saw these two incidents. Had he been a legislative analyst or a businessman he would have said that the popularizer was doing a useful job and should be advanced and the chairman had been grossly incompetent and should be sacked (he did in fact cease to be chairman, but he remained a respected scholar and teacher on the faculty). Why the differences?

The scholar sees the university as a community, although he might hesitate to use that word in public. The legislative analyst, on the other hand, sees it as an organization. Let me expand on this distinction, and justify its application.

The man wanting advancement was dismissed as a 'popularizer' and I imagine that 99 out of 100 academics would react with the same scorn. The contempt in which a 'popularizer' is held, particularly when he is himself a member of the academic community, comes about for several reasons. Firstly, he is using the discoveries of other people to make money or reputation for himself: the fact that special talents are needed to market the stuff (so that in fact he does add something), is usually ignored. Secondly, in the process of popularizing he is likely to dilute and distort: the fact that dilution may be a necessary price for the dissemination of knowledge is ignored. Thirdly, at the back of all this, lies a dominating myth among academics about their own superiority. Knowledge, for whatever reason accessible only to the few, is by that very fact superior to knowledge accessible to anyone. It is all strangely economic: knowledge is valuable in proportion to its scarcity.

In fact this argument is never taken to its logical conclusion, at least by scholars: for the conclusion must be that any sharing of knowledge dilutes it. But that will not do, since, by definition, knowledge (as distinct from mystical experience or revelation) exists only to the extent that it is disseminated, that is, shared with other people.[1]

The point must be that once the private language (the hieroglyphic) in which scholars talk to one another, has to be translated into the common speech, a threshold has been crossed. This threshold is the boundary between the community of scholars and the world outside. As soon as the secret language is translated, the *hoi polloi* are given the impression that they understand what is going on within the walls of the ivory tower and, it is generally assumed, will not be impressed.

The same myth of the community and its fragile sense of superiority comes out in the story about the ineffective chairman. Tall stories of this kind—they are to be found in abundance—constitute an almost proud proclamation of utter practical incompetence, and therefore of concern with higher things. I heard a chairman elsewhere say that he did not spend all those years in graduate school in order to use his talents in preparing budgets. The implication is that he could learn to do so if he wished, but in fact it was a task better left to less valuable people. Of course these stories of asinine ineptitude in practical affairs are a caricature, but caricatures are drawn to point a moral: and the moral in this case is that academics have special talents which, like the learning produced by those talents, are eroded and diluted by being brought into close contact with the affairs of the everyday world.

The two stories set the theme for this chapter. We began with three myths which contradict one another: a university is a collection of scholars who, whether individually or in small teams, keep their eyes down upon intellectual problems, and look nowhere else; secondly, the university is a community of scholars, who are answerable to one another and answerable not only as intellects but also as colleagues; thirdly, a university is an organization of experts providing a product for the world outside. This chapter is about the contradiction between the university as community and as organization.

Accountability and Tenure

A community is a collection of people who are expected to treat one another as full human beings, as ends in themselves, rather than as instruments. Of course, certain benefits are to be got or costs incurred from membership, but, as in the case of the family, membership is a matter of morality rather than of business. A community, unlike an organization, has no measurable product. One can talk of benefits like security or costs like the lack of privacy, but there should be no simple notion of material profit, as there is in the case of organizations like the Ford Motor Company.

The community as a whole is intrinsically valued; so also for members there is a relatively high threshold of accountability. Because there is no *single* criterion for excellence, if you are to be thrown out you need to get black marks for a long time and in a lot of places and with a lot of people and be classified, as Radcliffe-Brown put it, as a 'bad lot'. The judgement is one of the whole human being, rather than of a particular action.[2]

'Existing for its own sake' appears not only in the rejection of extrinsic criteria to justify the community's existence, but also in a more general reluctance to go in for codification and planning—indeed a suspicion of any form of open rationality. Act first and justify later: identify the goals by looking backwards and seeing what in fact has been done.[3]

Finally in a community many things are known but left unsaid. People are reluctant to make open and formal accusations, for which they must take responsibility. Opinions get bruited around through rumor and gossip. People are much concerned with saving face, others' as well as their own. This consideration is not shown to outsiders, for the relationship with them is instrumental rather than moral.

That these features exist in university communities is apparent in attitudes towards accountability and in the institution of the tenured appointment. To whom is the scholar accountable: to himself, to his fellow scholars, or to the world outside? The tenure system leans towards the first answer: the scholar can be trusted to discipline and evalute himself. But in most institutions this privilege is granted only after a rigorous inquiry into his qualifications to belong to the community of scholars. The candidate has to have proved himself by earning a good reputation as a scholar, has to have shown competence in teaching, and is expected to have put in service on committees or in other ways for the institution.

In some places still, and once more generally, this inquiry is conducted very much in the community mode, by the dean or his equivalent informally soliciting opinions from within and beyond the institution: things are arranged through highly personal networks, and there is much mutual trust: a man's nod or the shake of the head is good enough without further explanation, because the inquirer knows his respondent well enough not to have to ask what criteria he is using.[4]

In other places there is a different system. Although the Chancellor still has the last word, he is required to hear the advice of several reviewers, including a committee of the academic senate. This committee and the various *ad hoc* committees which it sets up, represent the community of scholars, both those on the campus and those in the discipline elsewhere. It exists to put into practice the ideal that standards of scholarship should in the hands of scholars, not in the hands of administrators, not even those on the campus, certainly not those who hold power in the world outside.

But every thesis has its antithesis: while set up to represent the community of scholars, the peer review committee follows procedures which, unlike those of the relatively autonomous dean, tend much more towards the spirit of an organization than of a community. For example, it insists on evidence: if the sponsoring chairman asserts that the candidate is a popular teacher, the file must contain evidence from students that this is so: when references are solicited from outside the campus, more weight is given to those who know the candidate only through his published work, and less to old friends, old teachers, and former colleagues. It is indeed a paradox that admission to membership of the community is granted by relatively bureaucratic and organizational procedures.

Neverthless, on balance tenure is an indication of the myth of the community of scholars. While, as I will explain in a moment, the granting of tenure does not entirely liberate one from the strains of being accountable, it does immensely extend one's credit. Just as in Radcliffe-Brown's primitive community the only crime against which public action is taken is that of being a 'bad lot', so the granting of tenure is equivalent to being judicially pronounced a 'good lot' and subsequent failures have to be both catholic and spectacular before the point of expulsion is reached. In brief, to grant tenure is equivalent to saying 'you are one of us.'

But again the organizational myth comes up as the antithesis. In that brilliant quip which has now become a cliché: we are all equal, but some are more equal than others. At some universities once tenure is achieved there are almost a dozen further steps through which a scholar may advance if he is considered to have sufficient merit. Every two years, and in the higher ranks every three years, the department is required to submit a file recommending either no change or advancement to the next step or, in exceptional cases, an accelerated advancement. The criteria are the same as for tenure: scholarly achievement, competent teaching, and service to the university and beyond. The procedure is the same: the committee which represents the community of scholars, together with some other reviewers, advises the chancellor about the department's request. There is the same reaching for impersonal and bureaucratic procedures: a strict form of accounting which is designed to encourage continued activity, so that the scholarly achievements used to move from one step to another are, so to speak, 'used up' and cannot be taken into account when the next move is under consideration. Furthermore, performance is supposed to get more impressive at each step, so that in theory it is difficult for someone who wins a Nobel prize and is accelerated from Step 2 to Step 4, to improve on his performance in order to get further in the system.

At that point the rules have reached absurdity, and the freedom to manipulate them, characteristic of the community myth, takes over again. The rule that performance must get progressively better at each step tends to be pushed aside in favor of a norm of equity: the man who won the Nobel prize at Step 2 can certainly be advanced so long as his performance is as good as that of the rest who already occupy the step to which he is being promoted. The abstract standard of some quantifiable attribute is made subordinate to a criterion which is the familiar 'he is one like the rest of us'.

If one reads the letters which are solicited from outside and supposedly impartial referees—and in the past two years I have read thousands—there is every indication that the spirit of community is at work, perhaps in nine cases out of ten. It is very rare that one encounters a negative letter. Those few that I have seen have usually been so extreme, so vituperative that the reviewers tend to write them off as an entirely community-like manifestation of personal dislike. The great majority of the letters range from favorable to effusively favorable, many of them neutralizing what impact they might have had, like tainted evidence in a court of law, through phrases which reveal a community-like connection which must blunt objective judgement: for example—and this is not fiction—'his father is my dearest friend'. The letter which cuts the knot, and it is a rare event, is one which assesses the work, points out what is good and what is not good, and balances out the two sides to make a recommendation.

One need not be surprised that this state of affairs exists, particularly at the senior level of each discipline, for there is in fact a community through which people get to know one another as persons, rather than solely through their scholarly productions. Indeed the letter of recommendation from a friend *of the enquirer* is effective, because one assumes (sometimes mistakenly) that friends do not unload their duds onto one another.

One suspects also that community values reassert themselves over the impersonal norms of organization through various ways of 'laundering' evidence. The departments solicit external references and it must happen occasionally that a referee's letter which goes spectacularly against the departmental opinion might get lost before the file emerges from the department. The peer review committees have the right to solicit reference letters directly, but rarely do so unless they suspect that for one reason or another the individual is being unjustly treated by his department.

In my experience, and this may of course be the accident of

acquaintance with a limited number of universities, such malice is rare, while the opposite—the determination to look after one's own, the somewhat weak and the somewhat deviant along with the rest—is the dominant sentiment. Once again the analogy is with a family, which should protect its members, whether or not it is prudent to do so—in particular the weaker members. The same sentiment appears when a member of the 'family' chooses to go outside to higher authorities in order to assert himself over other members of the family: this causes great distress, as when, in village India, men appeal from the decision of the village *panchayat* to the administration's court of law. If you do that too often, you are soon labelled a 'bad lot'.

The Siege Mentality

I described earlier that curiously nervous elitism, which combines a firm sense of one's own superiority with a conviction that there is no way in which outsiders can be made to acknowledge this superiority. If one were to go back before the disturbances of the 1960s and to make a traverse from most of continental Europe to the United Kingdom and then to the United States of America, the nervousness would be least apparent in Continental Europe and most apparent in the United States. The European universities were best compared to the baronial castle or the fortified monastery, impregnable upon a hill, receiving tribute from a tranquil, or at any rate powerless, peasantry on the plains around. American universities seem more like the stockade on the frontier, carrying on an uneasy and dangerous trade through a few friendly but probably untrustworthy natives, while the woods around are filled with savages who any night might burn the stockade down.

This sentiment of total trust in people like one's self, at least in face of the outside world, and a readiness to use instrumentally and an expectation so to be used by those beyond the moral community, is a clear indication of community sentiment. At least in the kind of universities about which I am talking (not the small community colleges), Town and Gown are not friends, but enemies.

One manifestation of this sentiment lies in the attitude of those in the 'core' segment of universities towards institutions which, by their nature, are brought into unusually close relationships with, and often are unusually accountable to, outside bodies. Departments of education, perhaps also some business schools, tend to be given second class status. The folklore says that scholars and teachers, who could not make it elsewhere, end up there. This is even said of medical schools, although the cleavage is within the medical school (between the clinicians and the researchers) rather than between it and the rest of the university: once again it is a sentiment on the part of the 'thinkers' that their way of life is at once despised and threatened by the 'doers'. I recall also the resentment felt for an institute for social research: the caliber of its staff was not, for the most part, in doubt, but they were said to do 'quickie' jobs, to be contemptuous of pure research, and they were also said to make a lot of money: in some ways they were very much like the 'popularizer', felt to be prostituting not only their own talent but also the standards of their disciplines in order to give the outside world what *it* wanted, rather than what it should be educated into wanting. Consistently, those research institutes which were not concerned with applied problems but served the pure ends of scholarship are regarded with respect: I spent seven contented, although underpaid, years in one such place and no one ever thought about being accountable to anyone or anything except the standards of scholarship.

Along with those sometimes less than honest manipulations over letters from external referees, there are other indications that, as in any community, instrumental rather than moral standards apply when dealing with outsiders. An example is the meeting of a relatively large number of people, the chairmen of departments and various other executive and partly-executive persons: about sixty or seventy in all, and in no sense the four or five conspirators in the back room. The problem on this occasion was a rule imposed on the university from above by the University Grants Committee following a formula set by the Ministry of Education, that the amount of public funds available for buildings should be governed by the amount of space used for teaching students. It therefore paid the university to occupy for every possible hour every possible inch of formally designated classroom space. Underuse would make it impossible to extract building subsidies from the state. On this occasion someone from the planning office produced a document, which, having explained that classrooms were available from 7:00 in the morning until 10:00 at night, informed his audience that most teachers tried to get their classes somewhere between 10:00 in the morning and 4:00 in the afternoon. The meeting was well disposed towards this young man and somewhat lubricated by sherry, and this far from startling news was greeted with encouraging noises which went on until the speaker revealed that 30 per cent of all teaching was time-tabled, at the request of the teachers, in spaces that were *not* formally designated classrooms. There was a sudden silence; then the chairman said, quite sharply 'Fix that figure! I don't mean make people teach in different places; that would be a lot of trouble. I mean just fix the figures, before they go up from here.' Then, like a Greek chorus, almost all those present started saying, 'Fix the figure! Fix the figures!'

Remember that this is a gathering of more than sixty people, all apparently united in a criminal intent to launder the evidence in order to extract greater resources from the world outside.

This does not, of course, imply that communities will attempt to cheat the outside world and that organizations will not: clearly that is not true. The point rather is that a very large number of people within organizations are perfectly willing to cheat the organization, whereas in the community—and universities have this characteristic—cheating within the boundaries is a sin; putting one over on outsiders is not. Figures on classroom space can be fixed; figures on one's experiments cannot, because that would be to deceive one's fellows.

We now pass from these rather generalized statements about attitudes, to a description of some myths about personnel.

Personnel

My personnel are divided into three categories: the chairmen of the departments, the senate, and the academic administrators, and in this chapter I deal with the last two. Of course there are others on the scene: other administrative and executive personnel, research workers and technicians and specialists who are not senate members, and, most important, the students. But they must wait for another occasion.

The senate and its committees represent, above all, the community of equals. There are committees on privilege and tenure, on academic freedom, on welfare, on educational standards and programs, on graduate study, and a personnel committee to which I refer elsewhere, which deals with appointments and advancements. In addition, there are other committees of a more executive nature, designed to keep the business of the senate running smoothly.

The senate myth about itself has come out, to some extent, in our discussion of 'community' and of 'scholarship'. Of course, there is cynicism, and academics are given to self-mockery, but when the announcement has to be made from the pulpit it concerns scholarship, the gaining and transmission of knowledge to other scholars and to students. Research and the sharing of knowledge are ends in themselves, requiring no further justification, and we alone—not the departmental chairmen and not the academic administrators—are equipped to decide what particular pieces of work reach these standards.

The senate is a highly public body, working very much out of the front office and it is inconceivable that one should ever hear shouts like 'Fix the numbers!' in the senate. Senate members try to look after their own, but they do so by insisting that rules should be equitably applied, rather than by the manipulations characteristic of 'community' behavior.

The senate caricature of the academic administrators portrays them as unconcerned with the true objectives of education. They pay lip service, but in their hearts regard debate about the ends of education as unproductive, unrealistic, and irrelevant, and they like to distinguish between good and bad by the simple criterion of the magnitude of resources. In a phrase which has become notorious on my own campus, the good department is the one which 'sells the most tickets': the one most in demand by students, because this also is the criterion used by the university's paymaster, the governor and the legislators. Consequently, popular teaching (whether successful or not is another matter) attracts the largest share of the resources. From this point the myth proceeds by easy steps into deciding that administrators are interested in acquiring resources and power, as ends in themselves, even at the cost of good scholarship. The distinguished scholar who is an indifferent teacher of undergraduates or, worse, contumaciously indifferent, has to be very distinguished indeed before the administrators consider him an asset to the campus.

Thirdly—and very much in the steps of Lewis Henry Morgan—an administrator tends to be autocratic and authoritarian, and if checked he becomes devious and manipulative. For example, when consultation is required by the university's regulations, very often the time allowed is so ludicrously short that those consulted feel themselves to be a 'rubber stamp'.

The administration's picture of senate members is no less unflattering. In its opinion they are given to inconsequential debate about policy, they are heedless of implementation, they are unrealistic, unable or unwilling to perceive that if they do not trim their sails to the prevailing winds, the ship cannot move at all. At worst, they are lazy and cynical and cunning and evasive, quick to vanish into the woodwork, and they raise a facade of scholarship to escape doing the job they have been paid to do.

The administrators also have a myth of themselves and their activities. Put them on the pulpit, and they talk a language acceptable to the community of scholars, the discovery of new knowledge and its dissemination. But, depending on the congregation and the occasion, they tend to take a further step and to explain that such activities are for the benefit of the people at large, the nation or all humanity. They like to make much of the practical benefits accruing from the applications of research and little is heard of the sheer intellectual curiosity the satisfaction of which is the researcher's true reward. The spotlight tends to fix more on teaching than on research (anyway at the present day and with the exception of certain fields, for example, medical research) and more on the benefits that will accrue to a non-university public than to the world of scholarship.

To a more restricted audience administrators will say that they are gatekeepers; they let the good things in and keep out what is harmful. Unlike the scholars they are the realists and, as a father must protect his family, they protect the community of scholars, keeping it in existence in the face of a largely hostile world, with which the scholars themselves do not know how to cope.

There are, then, two partly opposed myths. For the senate, the problem is to preserve the standards of scholarship by controlling an executive which has an imperfect understanding of these standards and is always likely to be corrupted by power. For the administration the problem is to preserve the standards of scholarship by adapting those standards, in the teeth of an unrealistic and obstructive senate, to the realities of the world outside. For each contestant, the more the other gains power, the greater the risk to knowledge and its dissemination. In short, the senate and the administration are locked in a continuing contest to impose on each other their own version of the reality in which they live.

The Budget and the Plan

I will conclude this chapter with two examples of the opposed myths of senate and administration being used to give meaning to events.

In a complex process the university puts together a statement of its needs for each year, together with their justifications. These are passed through the university's president to the regents, who then present their budget to the governor of the state. The governor in turn puts out his budget proposals, not just for the university, but for the entire state.

At the time when the governor had made his budget speech, but the details had not been printed, I attended no less than five separate committees (which included both senate members and administrators) at which one or another member of the planning or administrative staff gave an exposition of the governor's budget. This went on over a period of three weeks, and even on the last occasion, I noticed with surprise that the talk was prefaced by a statement that they had no *written* material about this budget, and the news had come either over the telephone or through informal meetings with contact-men in the university's higher administration. Of course, the information was probably firmer than hearsay, and much firmer than rumor, but it still seemed strange that they did not wait a few weeks until the information was made formally available. This is, after all, a bureaucracy, and a bureacracy is supposed to work on memoranda, on things in writing, rather than through the highly personal whisper down the telephone. Listening, one had the feeling of being admitted into a conspiracy.

Even more strange was a sense of uncertainty, conveyed perhaps unintentionally, a sense almost of slight panic, as when the engine of a car begins to misfire. All speakers stressed that this year they had not been able to get a single him beforehand of what would be in the governor's speech. Absolute secrecy had been maintained: in other words, those word-of-mouth contacts, effective in previous years, had this year failed them. At first I could not see why anyone should be much concerned about this, since it is in the nature of budgets to be kept secret until the moment for public pronouncement.

Evidently there were messages within messages. Firstly, it is obvious that the members of these various committees, including the senate members, were being admitted to the 'backstage' of the politics of administration: being given the privilege of getting the news before it was 'officially' available, and invited to join in the counter-planning, then being prepared to increase our share of the resources. We were being shown that our administrators had an effective set of personal links which enabled them to go behind formalities of front stage negotiation, and get things done. We were also being shown—perhaps inadvertantly—that on this occasion the links ('long arms' as the Italians call them) were not so effective. Finally, we were being told that although our administrators were able to go behind the scene and get things done in ways that are most politely described as unorthodox, they had honest intentions—always the good of our campus: continually either University Hall or the legislators were held up as the threat, the enemies, against whom we should all close ranks. Out of this studied uncovering of the personal networks which constituted one kind of reality behind the facade of formal negotiations, emerges clearly an invitation to adopt the administration's myth of itself (as benevolent and realistic), an implicit denial of the senate's myth of the administration (as self-interested), and a definition of one community which embraced both the administration and the members of the senate.

My final example concerns planning in general. Every three years the campus produces an academic plan, outlining its intentions for research and teaching, balancing out resources, and justifying these decisions. Since the plan concerns academic matters, by the rules of the university the final responsibility lies with the senate, which has not merely the right to give advice, but also power of veto. By the standards of those produced on other campuses our plan was apparently a model of its kind, but it had a very rough ride through the senate committees. Partly this came about because—as is not surprising—the planning staff had the thing fairly well baked before they offered members of the senate a chance to taste, and this together with an unfortunately short time for the review, caused the senate committees to think that this was just token consultation.

The plan itself also was disturbing. To senate members it exhibited only formal and empty statements about the aims of education and the search for knowledge. The overwhelming message was that the campus was doing a fine job with the resources it had, but needed more. There was no realistic description of difficulties faced and overcome, or difficulties anticipated; paradoxically, it was the turn of the senate members to say 'unrealistic'. These misgivings were deepened when administrators, being asked what fundamental assumptions guided the plan, replied that everything was negotiable. No one need fear that the plan would limit options to make claims on resources: no rights were being signed away by agreeing to this document. The senate members found this strange: a plan which is infinitely negotiable can hardly be called a plan. Of course, in the end, it turned out to be the senate members who were 'unrealistic' because they had not realized that this plan only *appeared* to guide the future allocation of resources on the campus: it was in fact mainly a bid to bring resources to the campus: first get the spoils, then divide them. The plan was not addressed mainly to the community of scholars, but rather was designed to 'educate' (that word was used) those remote people at University Hall and to provide them, in turn, with suitable materials to 'educate' the governor and legislators.

The senate members, mindful only of their own myth of themselves (for the substance of the plan) and their own myth about the administration (their annoyance about the method of consultation), had missed the point. The administration, from the beginning, had seen the plan in terms of their own myth about themselves: men who translate the values of scholarship to make them comprehensible and acceptable to people outside the community of scholars (a category which certainly included University Hall).

Conclusion

In this chapter I have outlined some myths available for use in university politics. They display two features. Firstly, on some occasions, and by some people all of the time, the university is regarded as an organization which employs scholars and pays them a wage, and expects to receive from them in return a product: profit (suitably defined) and accountability reign. On the other hand a university may be considered a community of scholars, who set up and maintain their own standards of good conduct, and who take on obligations towards one another which take precedence over any duties which they may have towards outsiders, even those outsiders who foot the bill: profit and accountability are nowhere and collegiality reigns.

Secondly, there is a distinction between what is done and said directly and openly in public, and what is kept more private. The public world deals with principles and policies (whether of community or organization) and the private world is a discourse about persons and the implementation of policies.

NOTES

1. This proposition goes partly into reverse in the case of those scholars (mostly natural scientists with a sprinkling of economists) who write their reports in the 'grey' or restricted literature. They do so for the simple and compelling reason that the sponsors of the research will not allow open publication. Other scholars look with a jaundiced eye on such activity, not because they share what seems to be the media phobia about confidential material, but because they suspect that such reports are not given thorough scrutiny by competent scholars, being restricted to a coterie of those who will be tempted to cover for one another.

The scientist whose file is filled with letters of praise from Washington bureaucrats and retired admirals falls into the same pit as the popularizer, not because he panders to the multitude, but because he goes to the opposite extreme and closes off his findings from his fellow-scholars. Thus they are left to suspect the worst; that his friends who praise his work, even when they are competent to make the judgement, will dull the sharp edge of their comments in the interests of friendship.

2. See *Radcliffe-Brown* p. xv.

3. This 'looking backwards' inevitably tends to have conservative results. Note that it is not an effort to restore a distant golden age, from which there has been a fall: there is nothing of the grand philosophical design implied in that notion, only a short-range grubbing around for the handiest precedent to justify an action or reach a decision.

'. . . except on rare occasions, the historic policy of the American college and university . . . (was) . . . drift, reluctant accomodation, belated recognition that while no one was looking, change had in fact taken place.' (Rudolph p. 491)

4. There is a quotation in *Murray* p. 173: *κοινὰ τὰ φίλων*, which most thriftily expresses this tacit confidence. 'Common are the things of friends:' in other words 'Friends require no explanations'.

CHAPTER THREE

Outsiders

The World Outside

Looking back on 1951 I now realize that I lived in a Garden of Eden: by 1974 there had been a Fall, but whether this is to be attributed to Sin or to Predestination (and, indeed, whether it is deservedly named Fall) remains a question.

In 1952, when first I went to India, those who paid for the research asked only if I seemed qualified to carry it out. They did not ask whether it was useful, or to whom it was useful. Whether that research was into contemporary social change, or an archaeological dig, or an inquiry into the structure of sixteenth century Tamil proverbs, no one seemed to care. We were to make a contribution to knowledge: no further justification was required. To raise questions about 'relevance', would have been to brand oneself as 'rackety', 'unsound' and a person likely to falsify the evidence.

Later enterprises in the mountains of Europe (in the mid-1960s) took place in altogether another world. In the climate of the times we felt ourselves compelled (although our prospective sponsors made no crude demands) to demonstrate that in the future Britain and Europe would be crucially damaged if we were not able to study the final phase of European peasant life. We connected our research with such pressing current problems as migrant labor, political instability in impoverished farming areas, the price of butter and any other fashionable concern on which we could lay our—by now rather dirty—hands: apparently knowledge was no longer an end in itself. But in fact this was a collusive game: those who gave us the money knew very well that the presence or absence, success or failure of a dozen graduate students carrying out anthropological research would have no effect at all on the price of butter and only the most indirect effect, if any, on problems such as migrant labor.

The Fall came in 1974. In that year I had the ultimate experience of listening to an administrator from an organization which previously had financed anthropological research announcing that unless we turned our attention—and at this point he produced a card from his pocket and squinted at it—to child beating or alcohol abuse or juvenile delinquency, we could go elsewhere for our funding. My first comment is that of another man pretending disenchantment: '*O Tempora*! *O Mores*!' which, in case you lack the Latin, means 'Everything has gone to hell.'

Further reflection, as you will see, denies the luxury of this extreme judgement.[1]

My theme in this chapter is that set of myths which we hold about the extent to which the life and work of a scholar is and should be connected with the world outside. Four myths will be compared. First is 'withdrawal': that a scholar's only concern should be with his own scholarly work, and he has no obligations beyond this. Second is the 'predatory' myth: this agrees with the goal of withdrawal, but recognizes the impracticality of that course and advocates extracting resources from the outside world without giving anything in return.

The third myth is that of 'commitment'. According to this the scholar's first obligation is to serve mankind, not only by scrutinizing continually and carefully the likely effects of new knowledge on the world, but also by setting the direction of research according to what the world wants. The fourth myth is 'adaptation', a complex affair, much the most difficult to analyze, but sufficiently described at this point as a loose combination of the other three myths, held together by the first rule of pragmatic living: whatever is desirable, only that which is practical is worthy of time and effort.

This set of contrasting myths contains a problem which far transcends the academic life. The point is that we live by cybernetics and without a steersman we are lost. 'Steersman' means those processes by which myths become adjusted to a changing reality, so that man can better shield himself from the pressure of that reality and at the same time exploit its resources. How do we set up trade-off statements for different kinds of values? Given that people have conflicting demands on their allegiances and their resources, what circumstances make them decide in favor of one rather than another claim? How much credit are you willing to lose with your family and neighbors in order to make a big name? How far will you risk alienating all the old people in the interests of modernity? How far, indeed, are you willing to trade off ends, thereby transforming them into means? It is, indeed, a ubiquitous question.

Questions which concern fundamental values clearly allow no single *reasoned* answer. My present enterprise is less ambitious, for it concerns not the relative value but rather the political use of such myths. The fourth myth, that of 'adaptation', stands apart from the other three. It more accurately reflects what in fact happens most of the time and it is characteristic of those who call themselves 'realists'. The other three myths start out from 'advocacy positions': they are rhetoric, not in the sense that those who voice them are necessarily insincere, but in the sense that they are designed to shape attitudes rather than to put forward plans which can be implemented. They are not programs for future action: they are ideologies. So also is the adaptation myth: but its holders pretend otherwise.

Withdrawal

The myth of extreme withdrawal appears in some of the novels of the 1960s, notably *Lucky Jim,* or in such books as O'Toole's *Confessions of an American Scholar,* which was published in 1970. This myth advocates withdrawal even from scholarship itself (or at least from its dissemination) and is epitomized in Oscar Wilde's statement quoted in the *Confessions* 'education is an admirable thing, but it is well to remember from time to time that nothing that is worth knowing can be taught'. Essentially this is the message of *Candide:* that most people (including the author) are ridiculous, that most institutions are sham, and that any effort in the direction of great things is without point. The hard way to do this is, like Diogenes, in a tub (in fact, following Gilbert Murray, it was not a tub but a large urn used for burial, the ultimate symbol of withdrawal from worldly obligation).[2] More commonly, those who proclaim withdrawal can afford, in the material sense, to do so: they have a private income, or a successful textbook, and not too many dependents.

The non-cynical form of withdrawal is from obligations to the world and from community responsibilities in order to devote oneself to scholarship. This is in the style of the *sanyasi*: not the morose and baleful glare on all around like Diogenes, but a search for personal salvation and redemption by achieving unity with a higher form of existence. This is a reasoned course of action and we have already met some of the justifications: Deans are appointed to be administrators, and they should be allowed to get on with it; those expensive years in graduate school were not intended to create petty administrators; and all those happy myths of the practical incompetence of scholars.

As in other cases of redemption, there are thorns along the path. There is a very narrow line between the *sanyasi*, whom it is proper to respect, and the person who is *sauvage,* unable or unwilling to take on the proper obligation to interact with others, a likely candidate for remedial training and political reorientation.[3] In fact, those who withdraw from community responsibilities must go some way in the direction of being judged a 'bad lot'. Consider the process of selecting people for committees; X is never put on a committee, because it is known that he is too bad tempered or too violent in his opinions.

But in practice the thorns are blunted. There are no real sanctions for the 'bad committee member' and if someone does not wish to serve on committees, such behavior is rewarded, for he is not asked. Neither does the deviant have to fear adverse comment or disapproval, because his behavior has a normative justification. In short, you can be *sauvage,* because the institution does have a kind of 'product' (private scholarship and research) which can be used to cancel out the 'crime' of being non-cooperative.

The brute fact, of course, is that not everyone can follow this path. Those who withdraw proclaim themselves, in a very literal sense, *in statu pupillari,* orphans dependent upon some larger community (except, of course, for those few who have private means to support their chosen way of life).

Predators

Those who hold the predatory myth are seldom straightforward. Only in relatively private gatherings, at the present time anyway, would such a nakedly instrumental ideology be proclaimed. The predatory style of life is defended in two ways: firstly the plunderers, by reason of their superior calling, merit the spoils; secondly, the plundered are so manifestly inferior that no sin is committed by exploiting them. Alternatively, they are so stupid that they do not realize that spoliation is for their own benefit, and it would be pointless to try to explain to them, as distinct from assert, this fact.

Undoubtedly, I have made the case more crudely and in more straightforward language than one is ever likely to hear. For reasons that are obvious, the penalties for saying such things in anything but the most involuted sociologese make people cautious. Furthermore, given that strong ethos of community, discussed earlier, it would be unnecessary to speak openly: there is no need to justify this position, for the exploitation of outsiders is merely a transformation of the incontestable 'blood is thicker than water'.

For some people plundering becomes a way of life. Working at devices for putting one over on the world outside can become a full-time occupation, an end in itself. The mere gaining of resources displaces whatever was the end for which they were originally sought. This, you will remember, was part of the senate myth on the nature of the administrator.[4]

How does one recognize such people? Firstly, they are likely to define themselves as 'realists', and with reason in comparison with those who advocate withdrawal, since at least they recognize that there is an outside world. In the appropriate surroundings verbs like 'fix' and 'launder' are readily used. The outside world is presented as never benign, but rather as dangerous and malevolent and obtuse, the last being a fortunate characteristic in that the outsiders either fail to detect lies or cannot work out what should be done about those lies. For example, the peer review committees should tacitly put aside standards of scholarship, in the case of all but the most manifestly half-witted, and advance everyone through the system as rapidly as possible. They are our colleagues and we belong to one community, and the money, anyway, comes from outside the community.

Whether or not you approve of this morality, this myth has weaknesses when used as a guide for action. The most successful predators are those who are abundantly stronger than the people whom they plunder. The marauding brigands very likely get what they want out of unarmed peasants: the same peasants give as little as they choose to the beggar. In fact the predatory myth in the academic world is distributed neither among brigands nor among beggars, but sits easiest on those asses who forget they have no lion skins.

The Myth of Commitment

The academic *sanyasi* climbs into the ivory tower and away from the world of practical men. By contrast the committed man withdraws from scholarship into the world, thus reversing the last three Hindu stages of life: he increases his obligations in the world as he gets older.

Who is likely to take this course? It may be that certain fields of inquiry fail to sustain hope and curiosity beyond the early years. Certain kinds of mathematician and some other theoretical scientists, if they have not made their name by the age of thirty-five, become inclined to look for their satisfactions elsewhere, perhaps in administration. A colleague, himself an historian, claimed that some historians may go the same way, because once that first brilliant book has been written, there is nothing to do but to write the same brilliant book over and over again, and the restless mind will not be content with this. The point is probably not that such alienation is more common in the academic world than in other walks of life, but firstly that we are apt to talk about it more, and secondly, unlike the worker on the assembly line, we started out with the expectation that this was going to be not 'just a job' but rather a way of life, with its own intrinsic satisfactions. Attraction turns into repulsion and away we go to become Diogenes or deans or chairmen of departments or assiduous committee men; all this for want of the better thing that we would like to have done.

Such people can hardly be called committed, for the word implies a moral enthusiasm that in their case is lacking. This enthusiasm is found when the scholar develops a 'conscience' and a determination to use his knowledge and his skills not so much to bring order to a disorderly intellectual universe (which is the strictly academic endeavor) but in order to straighten out a disorderly *social* world. At the present time a small number of very distinguished scientists have in practice withdrawn from their disciplines in order to consider the social 'relevance' of those disciplines. I do not mean those reputations which back up like the drains and overflow into other disciplines: the richest examples being found in the social and political commentaries provided by surgeons, heavy with public renown and keeping the scalpel sharp only for the royal abdomen. Rather, I am thinking of the person who, quite suddenly, often as the result of some traumatic experience, realizes that what he could discover or what he has discovered has or could have an effect on the world. The remote and ineffectual econometrician switches suddenly into Third World development economics (where he finds himself in danger of drowning in the strong currents of politics and cultures, the existence of which he could formerly ignore). The best known case is the 'atomic conscience' which propels scientists out of the laboratory and into the Institute or Conference Room, in an endeavour to make sure that what they made into a sword can be turned into a plow share.

This myth claims that the scholar's duty is to enter the world, to provide leadership and services. In some cases these are personal choices and not offered as a way of life to be followed by every scholar. Others can stay behind and keep alight the flame of pure scholarship. Those who choose to go into the world are like Benedictine monks who went out from the Abbey to teach the wild people of the forest how to cultivate and how to clear the land. They are altruistic people, and have a mission and in no sense are they 'consultants' who deal with 'customers'. Like the Benedictine monks they lie on hard beds: they find it difficult to translate their knowledge into a language which the heathen understands; even worse, they discover that there are several other relevant areas of knowledge (like political science and public administration and economics and sociology) about which they are cripplingly ignorant. The point, of course, is that the most successful politician or administrator is not likely to be the man with the sharpest analytic mind. Nevertheless, despite these deficiences, these people set out to guide the world. In doing so, they still retain that sense of academic superiority: the world, so to speak, is their orphan; they must look after it. They are the Guardians.

The second form of commitment has quite another view on the status of scholarship. It is a set of techniques. Scholars are mere technicians whose job it is to serve a higher non-scholarly end, even at the cost of violating some guiding principles of the Academy: like not cooking the evidence. The sociologist, for example, in the service of a political party, so constructs his questionnaire that it will reveal not what attitudes people really hold, but rather those attitudes which the party thinks it expedient for them to appear to hold. This is Question 1 in the fluoride campaign: 'Do you agree that people should be allowed to poison drinking water?' Statisticians can prostitute themselves in the same way, serving up whatever figures will further their patron's cause. The list is endless: think of your favorite discipline and you will have little trouble in recalling how it has been, or working out how it could be, prostituted.

Selling out your principles in order to make your life more comfortable is something which your enemies do, but not your friends. If the latter choose to serve a political party of some powerful patron, it is because they believe in the cause. The common element is that, whether squalid or honorable, there is the same willingness to sacrifice the ultimate values of scholarship (in this case truth) to serve a cause.

The same kind of myth exists also in relation to the values of community, which can be betrayed and endangered by an excessive willingness to rock the boat, using leverage from the outside world. To use God's gift of a powerful personality and a connection with the world's militant oppressed in order to make universities more readily serve those oppressed people is a form of commitment somewhere between that of the man with the 'atomic conscience' (who believes that knowledge will help humanity) and the meretricious expert who will sacrifice professional standards in order to serve outside causes.

Rhetorical Themes

The portraits so far have been on the side of caricature. Granted even that these are myths (people and situations rendered simple so as to point at a moral), they are markedly lacking in subtlety.

The university is an ivory tower. Gown may have Town around it, but Town exists to service Gown in the way of an adequate number of grocery shops and tailors and bookshops and places to eat and to drink. That is the first myth.

The second myth states that it is the duty of the people to support learning, because learning is a superior thing, and if ever the people forget that, then the scholars have a right to go out and seize what they need.

Thirdly, it is the mission of the universities to change and improve the world, by making knowledge available for the use of the world, by providing education for those previously denied the privilege, in short by being active and concerned and committed. These things are done in the spirit of *noblesse oblige* and from a posture of superior wisdom.

Fourthly, we have no divine mission in the world and no obligation to provide leadership, but merely to serve as technical experts and consultants, instruments for other people to use.

Fifthly, connections with the world outside are used in order to advance one's career within the university.

You will have noticed how easy it is to slip from the light to the dark side of these descriptions. The man in the ivory tower is serving the true ends of scholarship: alternatively, he is a parasite behaving as if the world owed him a living. The committed man works to change society for the better: alternatively, he is presuming on his own superiority and offering guidance in areas where he lacks the required knowledge; alternatively, apparently committed to helping the underprivileged, he is merely using them in order to advance his own career.

It seems clear that seldom, if ever, is any *one* of these myths an adequate description of any man's performance. It might be possible to cobble together selections from each in order to describe an actual person, but it would be wrong to do so because they are not botched-up and over-simplified objective descriptions of some reality, so much as persuasion, attempts to make a definition of a person or a situation prevail so that people will act in one way rather than another. It would also be a mistake to think that that because these myths bear, at best, an imperfect relation to some objective reality, they are therefore unimportant: on the contrary, if you can persuade people that the myth they have held on faith and without question no longer can give them the resources which they desire, and at the same time you can elevate another myth to the required level of sacredness, you have changed the world.

Myths of Adaptation

This set of myths purports to describe reality. Four parts in five are pessimistic, in that essentially it says that there is no point in talking very long about the way the world should be: rather concentrate on the way the world is. The reason is that the world is large and intractable and amorphous and even if you have a grand design to which everything should conform, in practice you can at best expect to change only a bit at a time. If you push hard at one or another radical solution, the only result will be chaos. Change is always peripheral, and that is just as well because what really matters is left intact; alternatively, if fundamentals are changed, then the process has to be very gradual.

Although at most times and in most places, this myth is a more accurate description of reality than the other three, it is itself also an advocacy myth. In essence it advises stalemate between the other three myths, tempered by the capacity to elevate one myth and depress others according to the way the wind is blowing from the world outside. This is the myth of compromise and trade-off between the eternal verities, where ends and means may change places, but only very slowly or very discreetly so that people can go on pretending that what was really sacred before is still sacred.[5]

How does this myth depict the relations between the university and the world outside? Certainly the ivory tower is unrealistic, for most universities do not have the resources to withdraw from the world. Resources must come from outside, but since there is no king or bishop or other patron who will provide these sources solely as an act of piety, and since we are not strong enough to be brigands, then something has to be sold to the world outside, so that we can generate enough income to do what we want. But selling is not the same as selling out and an important part of our activities (both in relation to scholarship and to the community of scholars) must be kept free from control by outsiders.

Controlling the Market and the Customers

The myth of adaptation, which sees universities as necessarily involved in marketplace transactions, includes various strategies which guide marketplace activities: like most men of affairs, we have ways of rendering competition in the market less than perfect.

I will mention, but will not here discuss, the increasing failure to prevent ourselves from flooding the market with our talents. One suspects we are about to see more guild-like activities, restricting the entry of apprentices: and it will be interesting to see how this will be done, or rather how it will be presented, in a self-proclaimed open society. We may do it by raising the standards: the market may do it by diminishing the rewards.

It is unusual for academics to look on the world outside in this rather raw free-market fashion. More commonly, the attitude is that of the advertising men who see the world as a set of people who have to take on a set of beliefs about the product, and advertising is needed because the product will not sell itself. Difficulties arise because the immediate paymasters are seen to be part of a formal bureaucracy, which, like a commercial organization, thinks in terms of profit and loss, and which insists upon some measurable product as its standard of accountability. So we get those curiously inadequate but disastrously important ratios like undergraduate degrees per head of faculty, contact hours per week, volume of publication, frequency of citation,[6] and what not other crudity.

From the academic side, although something is learned from such figures (like who is past his peak and who is not pulling his weight in the community) none of them seems to address what matters in the world of scholarship. So, ways are found either to soften these demands or to appear to meet the organizational criteria without in fact doing so.

For example, attention is paid to generalized impression management, so as to give the taxpayer or the parent or the legislator the impression that value is being given for money. There are newspapers and cultural performances and vice-chancellors for public relations and radio stations and extension courses and an access of despair when the local newspaper publishes letters about long-haired male drug takers living on welfare with girls who have abortions and all of them students.

Another way of softening the hard edges of bureaucratic accounting is to develop community-like contacts with those who man the bureaucracy and with the controlling politicians.

In other words, one looks for a patron, who will accept one into a tenure-like relationship and not keep asking what he got for his money last week. Such patrons, when they are politicians of stature, are useful since one can point to those other politicians of the far right or far left who proclaim the predatory myth and seem to be able to advance their careers by attacking intellectuals in general and universities in particular, and say, 'Sick him!'

Thirdly the planners and statisticians have a special role in prostituting their talents for the benefit of the community of scholars by pretending to measure what is often unmeasurable. They succeed, providing that the other planners and other statisticians in the employ of the higher level of the bureaucracy and of the politicians, collude in this game—and while it may be in their interests to pick small holes in the edifice, it would be foolish of them to pull it down around themselves by saying, as Eli Devons did, that it was all magic, mere sleight of hand.[7] I will have more to say about this later, since the planners and statisticians play a similar role within the community of scholars.

Controlling the Community

Ideally, an organization, since it is run on reason, can adapt itself readily and efficiently to a changing environment. For a community, on the other hand, the typical reaction to changes in the environment is to build the wall higher. The myths of adaptation recognize this and include a number of strategies through which the irresistible force from outside can meet the immovable object of scholarly standards, without disaster. The men in the middle of this, as we saw earlier, are the academic administrators and their staffs.[8]

Some of these outside forces are like the rain: you can control it by putting up an umbrella or going inside but you cannot turn it off. So the rise and fall of birth rates and their effects upon the university enrollment are forces to which one must accommodate. Not far from the same category are such other 'accidents' as the personality and interests of whoever governs the state in which the university is situated, or of the Minister of Education, or of the policy of the federal government in funding research. But of all the four myths this one alone recognizes the inevitability of such forces and suggests ways of coping.

When it comes to getting in out of the rain, the administrators (let us agree to have them be the typical characters of the myth of adaptation) have difficulty in persuading some of their charges to come inside or to put up their umbrellas. There are two sources for these difficulties. Firstly, it very often happens that invitations to come in out of the rain are interpreted as demands to lower the standards of scholarship. For example, suppose that a university is required to admit a certain upper percentage of all high school graduates in the state. A proportion of these, which may be alarmingly large, and although sometimes brilliant in other ways, turns out to be unable to express itself in ordinary written English. They fail a test and the state requires that the university provide remedial education. This becomes a Cinderella, since most of the faculty feel that they did not spend 'all those years in graduate school' in order to do the kind of teaching that should have been done anyway in high school. We will see later what solutions are available. Another example is the so-called inflation of grades which has moved the average from 'C' to 'B', partly because aggressive students demanded this, partly because 'committed' faculty connived, partly because during the years of the recent war low grades could mean being drafted into the army. A third example is the creation of activities which most faculty regard as 'sub-university', interdisciplinary programs which seem to pander to whatever is the fashionable concern of the moment and to sprinkle 'A's around like grains out of a pepper pot. All these attitudes do not make it easy for the administrators to satisfy demands from outside the community of scholars.

Secondly, since there is a tenure system, they cannot easily accommodate by dismissing those faculty members whose minds are made up to resist, and putting in their places more pliant people. If there is to be a force available to meet new demands or exploit new opportunities, the only way is to create and hold in reserve a number of appointments. I describe later one scheme for creating such a 'pool' and the contempt which it aroused. The open suggestion that one should manipulate fellow members of the community in that fashion was pronounced by most of those present to be outrageous.

The myth of adaptation suggests ways out of these difficulties. As you will see, most of these ways seem to involve secrecy and duplicity and a rather sophisticated strategy which is designed to allow the administrator simultaneously to run with the hare and hunt with the hounds. The reason for their reluctance to manage these affairs in public arises from familiar sources: the more things get done in the open, the coarser are the moves made, and the greater are the possibilities of everything dissolving into the chaos of outright conflict. The myth of adaptation says that the greater the number of people admitted to the discussion or the contest, the higher becomes the proportion of those who are not only incapable of reasoning but are also unreasonable by nature.

One solution is to create a covert hierarchy. Everything which is new and is thrust upon the university from outside and is also unacceptable by the canons of traditional scholarship is put into a special inferior category. Remedial English is left largely in the hands of temporary lecturers and graduate assistants. Interdisciplinary programs are said to end up either in the hands of those who are not going to be successful in their own disciplines anyway, or, as in the other case, made the responsibility of temporary teachers hired from outside the community of scholars and certainly not admitted to full membership of it. Prophecies, in such situations, are likely to be self-fulfilling, and, with a few striking exceptions, such programs and their teachers meet the fate of mixed breeds and marginal creatures anywhere: derision, fear and contempt.

From the point of view of the administrator, the men in the ivory tower should be grateful because the infection has been kept outside the walls. By creating an academic caste system,[9] the purity of scholarship has been preserved from contamination. But as usual, the myth held by scholars refuses to recognize that they are receiving any favors: on the contrary, this is all a plot by the administrators to keep resources under their own control, so that they can use them to change the nature of the university by debasing its standards of scholarship: in other words, a version of 'divide and rule'. The remaining myth, that of the committed, sees it all as a half-hearted attempt to meet the legitimate demands of a larger society, a token enterprise, contained and rendered ineffective by the mean coalition of conservative scholarship and a power-corrupted administration. Against this, the administrators can only say that this is as far as they can realistically go in the direction of meeting the legitimate demands of the wider society.

In short, any fact (for example, that 7 per cent of the teaching staff are hired on temporary contracts) can be made to fit any of these conflicting interpretations. This is rendered possible because those who have taken the decisions, the administrators, in accordance with the myth of adaptation do not consistently and publicly commit themselves to any single point of view, to the exclusion of others, unless it is so abstract and so transcending as to be effectively without content. They are versatile men and that is their strength, and if you ask them what they believe in, the answer is 'Excellence!'

Even the smallest of private gatherings, however, never entirely drops its normative facade. No administrator boasts, even to another administrator. of being like Proteus. Versatility must be hidden so that all concerned can pretend that decisions, although apparently arrived at in a devious fashion and mutually inconsistent, are nevertheless worked out by the application of consistent principles, which are generally accepted. There are several ways in which this is done: one exploits the myth that those employed in universities will accept sound reasoning, even if they do not like the conclusion to which it leads: the second uses the myth of community, that to stand openly on certain principles in defense of scholarly standards will destroy the community, whereas in fact it is only necessary to *appear* to stand on those principles.

Given that academics are less likely than most people to say 'I don't care whether it's in accordance with the facts and figures or not; that's the way I want it!' they are helpless before anyone who can manipulate a code the authority of which academics accept but the details of which they cannot understand. It is not simply a matter of knowing statistics; many academics have that skill. Rather it is a substantive matter of knowing the appropriate statistics; of having the time and the opportunity to collect one's own statistics, of having the records of what went on last year and the year before, of being in contact with other planners at higher levels, and above all of doing this for the whole of the working week. Time and again I have seen meetings endeavoring to divide this year's resources among departments unnerved and unsettled by the suspicion that the pot was in fact larger than they had been told, and dissolving eventually into chaos because everyone had a different memory of who was promised what last year, and rescued eventually by one of the planning staff who emerges like God to end it with a divine Revelation. In short, logistical statements get to have the status not only of constraints, against which it is pointless to go, but even acquire an element of moral rightness, for to go against them is to go against the canon of rational behavior. In this way, through having better access than others to logistical information, the administrators are sometimes able to present what are in fact bargains and compromises as if they were the product not of competing interests but of reasoned thought. The unstructured dealing typical of a rigged marketplace is concealed behind a facade of logistical inevitability.

Finally, the myth of adaptation also contains covert appeals to community sentiment, which make the pill of innovation not more palatable, but more readily swallowed by those otherwise ready to die in defense of scholarly standards. I have several times heard discussions of affirmative action and of increasing teaching at the possible expense of research (both of which were presented as imperatives from the world outside) discussed not in terms of their justice, but in terms of the penalties: 'You'll get hurt if you don't.'[10] This is convenient in several ways; a potentially disruptive debate is avoided; secondly, precisely by avoiding this debate, the *moral* status of these imperatives is left unconsidered, and so the way is left open for discreet laundering and for following the letter rather than the spirit.

At first this seems mere cynicism. But, on reflection, it is just this deviousness and this double-talk and double-think which hold intact the center. Adaptation is a rational process: it requires the ability to learn from experience and the capacity to abandon articles hitherto accepted on faith. But this capacity is limited. Indeed, if it were not, we would live in such a state of flux that we would not live at all. Much of the adaptive process consists not in bending our faith to fit new experiences, but in pretending that these experiences are not new at all. The stability of our lives depends in part on making myths: on being able to create an agreeable facade in front of an ugly reality, and being able to make other people collude with us in pretending that this facade *is* reality, or at least is as near to it as a sensible person should get. Consequently, myths need just the right degree of sacredness: too little and the system dissolves into chaos because reality flows in too fast; too much and the myth is ineffective as a guide to action because it refers to a reality that no longer exists.

NOTES

1. Once again I have not thought it my business to trace the antecedents of the different myths, in particular to find out which myth tended to prevail (in the sense of being most commonly voiced) at any particular time, and—a different question—which myth does history show to have been most frequently acted upon. Within my own lifetime, as the three anecdotes about funding exemplify, it has become much easier to treat the 'ivory tower' or 'withdrawal' myth with derision, and there are, one suspects, fewer people around who will voice it openly and with confidence.

One opposing myth argues that involvement is inescapable, that all academic changes and reforms (usually for the better) are the result of pressures (directed funding, Commissions of Inquiry, and so forth) coming from outside the universities. The case is well documented at least for recent times in *Kerr,* who adopts the manner of the scientist sorting myth from reality: involvement is the reality and the ivory tower is the myth (pp. 94–108).

The reader, however, should be cautious. Remember that Kerr was President of the University of California and notice how much of his book fits with the myths of administrators reporting on scholars (described in chapter 2 of this book). Kerr is, in fact, an advocate and not the first or only person to use that curious argument that goals should be pursued because their attainment is inevitable (presumably whether pursued or not). History is used for persuasion and the rectifying hand of governments and people, exercised through Presidents and Chancellors is no less mythic advocacy than is its opposite (that such people should keep their corrupting hands out of scholarship).

In fact the power of the scholars to bend the world of 'doers' to their will became enshrined in stories about that first source of funding described in my text. The money—so it was said—was made available by the British government, when they found out during the earlier parts of the Second World War that they lacked sufficient experts on the languages and cultures of the Far East, Eastern Europe and—inexplicably—India. So—the myth continues—even after the war, anyone who got money from this source to carry out research, had a field marshall's baton in his knapsack and a parachute in his briefcase. But if one looks at much of the work done, the tune seems to have been called by the scholars: a definitive work on fourteenth century proverbs in an oriental language; a stimulating study (for the few phoneticians capable of understanding it) on a peculiar combination of noises made in a remote mountain tract elsewhere; and a host of other topics that would make even the unsporting Proxmire hesitate to shoot such sitting ducks.

2. *Murray* p. 37. Withdrawal, in the case of Diogenes, did not represent indifference to the fate of mankind, that total concern with one's own salvation and despair of promoting the public good by public means which elsewhere in Murray (p. 119) is characterized unforgettably as a 'failure of nerve'. Diogenes had a lesson to teach and a philosophy to impart.

The scholar's withdrawal, of which I am thinking, is more fittingly represented in its non-cynical form. It is not so much the idea that the world is an intractable place, but that time spent acting in it or on it is time taken away from scholarship: it is a matter of opportunity cost. Such a choice, of course, has a significance for the world outside scholarship, not only in many obvious practical ways, but also on some occasions by what the withdrawal symbolizes. Those interested in the meaning of withdrawal could begin with an essay, celebrated among Indianists, written by Louis Dumont.

The complexities of the range between withdrawal to save oneself and withdrawal the better to inform mankind are well explored in *Burridge*.

3. For discussion of the *sanyasi*, see *Dumont*. A brief description of what it means to be *sauvage* is found in *Blaxter* (p. 123).

4. As ever in politics, the line is easy to draw: the difficulty is being sure on which side of it to place people and events. The resolute gainer of resources from the outside world—if that is his only or main claim to fame—gets written off like the popularizer described in chapter 2 or the man who publishes in the grey literature (see note 1 to that chapter), as someone who has a part-parasitical and part-symbiotic relationship with the true scholar. Of course, like the administrator, the would-be predator will think of himself as an indispensable facilitator, a very important person, indeed a leader. See the comment in *Kerr* quoted in note 8 of this chapter.

5. Talking of his 'federal grant universities' *Kerr* (p. 49) remarks, 'The universities most affected have been making largely piecemeal adjustments to the new phenomena without any great effort at an overall view of what has just been happening to them. Perhaps this was just as well—the transition was smooth precisely because it was not subjected to critical analysis.' The 'overall view' and the 'critical analysis' are perilous to the extent that they make people realize that the pillars of their faith are being demolished. The outcome will be resistance or uncertainty. *Kerr* is noticing the same phenomenon when he writes (p. 38), '. . . innovations sometimes succeed best when they have no obvious author'. In other words, by being anonymous the innovations themselves are likely to be without a name, that much the harder to notice, that much the less likely to be perceived as threats to fundamental values.

6. If you manage to get past the referees of your learned journal with a paper containing an egregious error, you will do wonderful things for your citation rating.

7. *Devons* pp. 135.

8. In *Kerr* (pp. 94–108) the argument is made that universities, in particular the faculty with its 'guild' outlook, are deeply conservative. But because they depend on the world outside, they cannot close themselves off and run their own affairs. So changes are introduced from outside and the

mediator in such events (in several senses of that role) is the hero-administrator. 'Someone must seek concessions among the many conflicting points of view on a complex campus, must find workable compromises; otherwise the campus is abandoned to irreconcilable non-negotiable demands on the one side and static resistance on the other; otherwise initiative is left in the hands of the fanatic reformers and the fanatic supporters of the *status quo*—the proponents are both extremes of no compromise.' (p. 144). Kerr does not go on to say how his heroes do the job, beyond listing the qualities which they require: '. . . judgement, courage and fortitude—but the greatest of these is fortitude since others have so little charity' (p. 40). Clearly Kerr is out to shape the reader's attitude towards Presidents and other Administrative types: if he were appointing a man to such a position he would very likely look for a fourth quality: such a man must be smart, if he is to succeed. 'Judgement' is too clean a word for the quality I have in mind.

9. The analogy intended is with north-western India, where communities have a relatively simple caste profile: or perhaps with so-called 'tribal' areas. Four-fifths of the population belong to one caste: on the fringes are the several groups which constitute the remaining fifth—despised but necessary providers of various services which the dominant group will not perform for itself, activities too polluting for the Twice Born (the tenured and those on a tenure-track).

10. For an incident of this kind see the story of Bert in chapter 7.

CHAPTER FOUR

Committees[1]

Characteristics

Committees have three characteristics: firstly they are a small group chosen from a larger number of people whose business they are transacting or whose interests they are representing; secondly the group is given specific tasks or concerns; thirdly it operates with a degree of privacy impossible for the larger group which it serves.

Consider first size. One can have a Town Meeting, open to every one, so long as the town is not too big. If one thinks of a nation, even a relatively small nation like Belgium, even very small ones like Malta, one can no more think of deliberations by an assembly of the whole population—that is, *effective* deliberations—than one can think of a tennis match with eighty-eight people on each side of the net. But one need not push things to these ludicrous limits: in the case of groups which physically can assemble, the larger they are the more difficult it is to avoid a free-for-all, in which orderly debate towards a conclusion is impossible and the chance of taking action does not exist. Moreover, as the numbers increase so also must the simplicity of the information: discussion moves from policies to principles and from there to slogans and the mindless (if sometimes very effective) symbolism of the advertising world. As size increases such a drift is inevitable. But going the other way, the process is not necessarily reversed: diminishing numbers facilitate the movement back from slogans to principles to policies to persons, but it does not necessarily free a small committee from formality, posturing and the discussion of principles.

Why is this? Certainly as you multiply the numbers present, so also you multiply the chances of including stupid people, opinionated people, unreasonable people and destructive people. Also, by increasing the size you increase temptation to pay attention to an audience. There was a recent television report of an administrator making a tour in a farming countryside. The camera caught him just too soon: he was combing his wispy hair across his bald patch. Finding the lens upon him, he flashed a toothy smile and slipped the comb into his back pocket. A number of thoughts, none of them charitable, arose. The first was that the teeth must be false too; the second was that he was much too old to display such vanity; thirdly, with all those important problems facing him, how could he be worried about his appearance; and, fourthly, since his mind was evidently more on his image than on the problems of his administration, whatever he said was going to be superficial and platitudinous. Of course, these are harsh judgements: everyone knows that the politician who loses his favorable image is likely to lose his job and even the best of actions are unlikely to speak loud enough to compensate for a complete lack of ballyhoo. But the point remains: the presence of an audience gets in the way of performing the task in hand, because the performers are tempted to forget about the search for the best solution and to look for the one that will make the most favorable impression on the audience.

Why does all this get in the way of taking action? Having an audience in mind, a man tends to take up positions and argue in terms of principles, and to back away from the compromises which are usually necessary for an agreed course of action. It is not impossible for this to happen in small groups, but, I argue, the readiness to compromise usually increases as groups get smaller, providing that—which is usually the case—the degree of privacy increases. Certainly the rule works without qualification when moving in the other direction: compromise solutions, in which principles are sacrificed, are generally impossible in large groups whose actions take place before the public gaze, unless it can be shown that this was no sordid compromise but rather conformity to a transcending principle.

There are no doubt other things to be said about the constraints which numbers set on types of action and their efficiency. In the present context, however, the focus is upon degrees of privacy—the absence of an audience—and it will be enough to assert that, usually but not invariably, as the numbers in a committee decrease so also does the incentive to play to an audience.

A second main consideration is that a committee bears a strangely ambivalent relationship towards its parent body.[2] It reports back, and etiquette usually demands that the committee indicate a subordinate position by referring to itself as 'your committee . . .' and ending the document with the phrase 'respectfully submitted.' Parent bodies may debate the report and accept or reject its recommendations, but when they choose to reject it there certainly is a feeling that matters are not as they should be. The effective committee becomes one which can steer the larger body, and it is possibly just this potential domination of the master by its servant that is reflected in the curiously obsequious language which etiquette demands in committee reports.

What is the source of this carefully concealed power? Some of it certainly comes from privacy and secrecy: not merely the subjective feeling of superiority which comes from knowing what others do not know, but more importantly having exclusive access to information required to make a practical and sensible decision. Every time the larger body refuses to take the advice of one of its committees, it runs the risk of falling on its face because it may not know the grounds on which the rejected decision was taken, and may not itself have sufficient information to make a more rational decision.

The reason why committees sometimes get to steer the ship

is that in one way or another, compared to the parent body, they are experts. Not only do they have more information; but also they are expected to concentrate on a specific and limited range of affairs, about which, given sufficient time, they become experts. Once again it is a question of restricted information: this time not because privacy is a requirement, but because members of the larger body do not have the opportunity or the time or, in some cases, the skills to make themselves masters of the required information. In this way committees have the same power as the man who repairs the television set.

There is one other important ambiguity about the role of committees. Secrecy, decisions reached objectively by rational debate, and a specialized range of activities, all point in the direction of organization or bureacracy and away from the community style of politics. Consider the common stereotype of 'the good committee man'. He is rational and tries to argue the facts without displaying his emotions. If you wish to avoid committee service, get yourself a reputation for losing your temper or—if you are male in our culture[3]—try bursting into tears: you may get what you want on that occasion, but your services as a committee man thereafter will not be in demand. You are expected also to follow some of the cardinal directions of a bureaucracy: following the rules and leaving out of account personal considerations. The good committee man also does his homework. Most of all he does not give pain to his colleagues by consistently seeing matters from a perspective which astonishes them. In short, he is expected to be a rather dull but very worthy servant of the institution.

This image of what is supposed to exist within the pinstriped suit, beneath the bowler hat, in the briefcase, the man toting a neatly folded copy of the London *Times* and a neatly rolled umbrella from Waterloo Station or Charing Cross to Whitehall, will not long survive experience on committees, at least small committees in universities. For one thing such committees often turn out to be a clearing house for institutional gossip: this certainly does not find its way into the minutes or onto the agenda, and it may not take place around the table. But while walking to and from the meeting, during the break for tea, during the chatter between items for business, and occasionally in the business itself, the reputations of those under discussion may get built up or hacked about, characters and abilities are discussed in the light of folklore and oral history, and, as one would expect, the full roundedness of the moral person becomes an item of information used in reaching decisions, which are supposedly taken on wholly impersonal grounds. I will argue that such committees cannot work effectively unless they use such information, without formally admitting that it exists.

Secondly, in those small committees which are designed to take or recommend action, just because they are nearer to reality than the larger assemblies, the unprincipled business of compromise behind the scenes—one of the main indicators of the community style—takes place. This in turn reinforces the need for secrecy, because there are no public principles—other than 'reasonableness', which means refusal to stand on principle—by which the decisions can be defended.

In short, through the device of privacy, committees become a curious blend of authority and subservience, of principled action and unprincipled compromises, and bureaucratic impersonality combined with concern for persons. The rest of this chapter will illustrate and further refine these features.

My argument is drawn from examining several committees, selected, like the famous example of those central African villages which were reached on a bicycle, by 'accessible sampling'.[4] They are in fact some of the committees on which I served during the year before I sat down to make this analysis. My interest is in identifying features through which a comparison can be made: how typical these features are of all the committees on this campus, let alone all committees, I cannot say. I have changed the names of some committees, not in the hope that my colleagues will thereby fail to recognize them, but as a mnemonic device for the reader. Here is the list.

First there are three large bodies. One is the Academic Council to which every regular faculty member belongs: that is, it excludes visitors and temporary appointments and research appointments. If everyone came, the meeting could be several hundred strong.

Secondly, there is a Planning Council, about thirty members, containing representatives from the Academic administrators (that is, those administrators who also hold membership in the Academic Council), other administrators (those in charge of finance, buildings, student welfare, and so on), representatives of the heads of departments, of the Academic Council, of the library, of the graduate students and of the undergraduates, and some others.

The third large body is the Chairman's Council. Of chairmen, there are about thirty, but the meeting in fact usually rises to almost sixty, because it includes some senate representatives, the Academic administrators and a sprinkling of other administrators.

Then we have two smaller bodies. One has about a dozen members, and is called the Academic Advisory Subcommittee, being a meeting of the chairmen of all the committees of the Academic Council. Secondly, there is a Planning Subcommittee, with about twenty members, which is in effect one of the steering committees for the Planning Council.

Finally there are two kinds of committee concerned with hiring and firing, advancing and not-advancing faculty members. One is the Personnel Committee, which has seven members: this committee sets up *ad hoc* committees, generally of five members, to advise it on particular cases: as the name indicates these committees dissolve after the particular task has been performed.

In brief, we are taking a sample of seven committees, looking for some of the features which will discriminate between them, and finding reasons for these differences.

Showmanship and Formality

Service during the same period on those committees (or councils—I will use the former word) made it easy to notice that people behave in different ways: one also hears remarks about the difference between one kind of committee and another. These differences (which produce three connected questions, to which I will come in a moment) will be linked with two kinds of variable. One of these is the task of the committee, as interpreted by the members: their own myth of what they are doing. The other is structural or situational and is identified by the analyst: committee members may or may not be able or willing to talk about these connections.

The first question is this: Do some members get away with putting on an act and behaving as if they are present not to solve a problem but to build a reputation? An indication that people have a license to perform is the frequency of sermonizing, speaking one's piece without bothering to connect it with what has already been said, repeating the preceding argument, failing to make a connection with the point at issue, excessive parading of principles and a corresponding disregard for questions of implementation. These are common forms of acting on the Academic Council: such behavior is more restrained, but also certainly present, in the Planning Council and the Chairman's Council. People do this, of course, at other committees (being showmen by nature) but it is less common in these committees and the threshold of intolerance is lower. Members of the Personnel Committee rarely play to an audience and if such behavior occurs on the Planning Sub-committee, it crosses people's minds that this must be some Machiavellian tactic, for no one on that committee could really be wasting time and opportunity by flashing his roll of counterfeit eternal verities.

The second question is about the degree of formality observed in committee procedures.[5] Is there a special language that must be employed in speaking? Is there a procedural expert present and do people draw one another's blood with the sharp points of Robert's Rules? Are there cries of 'Point of order!' and 'Let the minutes show . . .'? Is one required to talk to the chair only or will the members address one another directly? Etiquette flourishes in the Academic Council, which has its parliamentary expert. All the other committees are more informal and, if a procedural difficulty does arise, for example, on the Personnel Committee or the Planning Sub-committee, it will not be heralded by a cry of 'Point of order!' but by an informal remark, such as 'Can we do it this way or should we . . .?'

The third question concerns the substance of committee discussions rather than the etiquette of communication. Does the committee restrict itself in the kind of information used? Specifically, does it operate under rules of relevance analogous to those found in our courts of law? Or does it allow a free-ranging discussion, including folklore and gossip about persons, in the manner of the Indian village *panchayat*?

In short, there are some committees in which showmanship runs riot and success is measured by the applause from the gallery, where etiquette and formality and ceremonial reign, and where the talk is about high principles and eternal verities unanchored by gossip-like information about persons. Such committees are 'public'.

Task and Responsibility

In some committees the members feel that their work is important and is done effectively. In conversation they volunteer this opinion and they back it by regular attendance and by doing the homework required to participate effectively. The Planning Sub-committee and the Personnel

Committee are both of his kind; usually this is true also of the *ad hoc* committees.

More common on the lips of the academics is the other judgement, as in the case of the Academic Advisory Sub-committee. While no one, so far as I know, has ever said that it is unimportant, attendance fluctuates, and meetings never go beyond the time alloted, since people often schedule other appointments immediately afterwards and, murmuring an apology, get up and walk out. Two groups about which one hears most disparaging comment are in fact councils having the legal and usually final right to ratify or refuse to ratify proposals presented to them: these are the Planning Council and the Academic Council. Despite this, the latter in particular is described as 'just a talking shop': or 'a rubber stamp'. Its meetings often begin late, waiting for a quorum, and terminate because the quorum dissolves as the members head out to do other things.

Whether a committee tends towards the public or the private model, depends in part on how the members see their own activities. Those who think they take 'real decisions' which will have consequences and who do so from a position of superior responsibility, will be inclined to form themselves, as far as possible, into a private committee. Those who believe they take 'real decisions', but do so by debate between the representatives of different constituencies, will be pushed in the other direction. Let us see how these propositions fit the committees listed earlier.

Two of them disappear from the list because they take no decisions. Both the Academic Advisory Sub-committee and the Chairman's Council are occasions for the exchange of points of view and the sharing of knowledge about current events. Persons are rarely if ever the object of discussion in these committees and the discussion generally is about academic policy (in the case of the Academic Advisory Sub-committee) and about academic and managerial policy and its implementation (in the case of the Chairman's Committee).

The meetings of each of these groups are held so that people will be aware of each other's problems and will have the sense of being involved in what is going on. Members behave occasionally as if a strongly expressed point of view might have an influence on decisions taken elsewhere: indeed, this may happen. But in a formal sense neither the Chairman's Council nor the Academic Advisory Sub-committee ever takes a decision, and so this cannot be counted as a factor moving them towards the public or the private mode of behavior.

The argument, it should be made clear, is about the connection between members' ideas on whether or not their decisions will have important effects and the way they prefer to run their committees. There is no implication that councils and committees which exist only for consultation and involvement and even sociability, are unimportant: still less that bodies like the Academic Council or the Planning Council, because they are called 'rubber stamps', could therefore be abolished without cost. The ceremonial and ritual activity of the front stage as is well known, serves to proclaim fundamental values and to provide a sense of stability.

If the committee members think that what they do is important, one must then ask to whom do they feel they are accountable. This distinction produces two kinds of committees' 'elite' and 'arena':[6] in the former, members perceive themselves as guardians of the institution and its values, godlike in their responsibilities; the latter is made up of members usually in competition with one another because they are no more than the representatives of outside interests.

Elite committees, the members of which think of themselves as accepting responsibility for the collectivity and reaching a decision in the best interest of all, intrinsically value their own existence and tend towards privacy. Committees of specialists, sharing a particular skill and bringing it to the committee, or acquiring it in the course of their work, tend to see themselves in this fashion. They keep their own ranks closed against those whom they govern or advise. This kind of behavior is also true of those committees which turn out to be councils of war, which, in the face of some external opposition, feel the need to close ranks and to suppress sectarian differences.

The arena committee tends towards the public model. The members of the committee are representatives of bodies outside, to which they are accountable and to which they must report back, and the awareness of this potential audience will push members towards posturing and the language of principle and policy, and away from a gossip-like exchange about persons. Furthermore, since altercation has to be contained if anything is to be done, there may be a tendency to develop rules of etiquette, and with that would appear the suspicion that the committee's work is becoming ritual and ceremonial, leaving the real decision to be taken elsewhere. In practice, this descent and fall is usually arrested, because the contestants begin to see the necessity for collusion and for concealing from their followers some of the deals they make with the opposition. The Planning Sub-committee is an example: the crude antagonisms of its earlier days have been softened a little by increased formality but more by a growing *camaraderie* and spirit of give-and-take among the members.

The Personnel Committee from every point of view is an elite committee. Its members have no constituency other than the whole body of faculty. They acquire a specialized knowledge of the quite complex regulations under which they must operate, and, more important, a highly specialized folklore about the departments and their colleagues. There are also occasions when the Personnel Committee functions as a council of war: either against a recalcitrant department which seems to be treating a faculty member unfairly, or against academic administrators, who show signs of wanting to ignore advice. On this committee there is little posturing; there is little formality; there is no hesitation whatsoever in talking about persons; and the members tend to develop a magnified sense of the importance of the decisions they reach.

They are aided in this opinion by the folklore of the campus which looks upon this committee as powerful and somewhat mysterious.

The committee members' image of their task and its effect upon the way they run their business is influenced by the degree to which the main principles for making decisions are handed down as directives, either by a superior authority or by traditions sufficiently sacred to be beyond dispute. The greater part of the time of the Personnel Committee is taken not in arguing about what should be the standards for advancing a faculty member (these are set down in the regulations with great firmness and a deceptive clarity) but in considering whether or not particular people meet these principles and how best to make the enquiry. This has the effect of allowing the committee to retreat from principles and get on with its business, the front stage debate having been decided elsewhere. The Planning Sub-committee is less constrained: the principles on which a rational division of resources can be made between departments and others are far from clear and no one has found an agreed way to get from the desire to have a most distinguished university (about which everyone agrees) to deciding what this should mean, for example, in dividing resources between the natural sciences, the social sciences, and the humanities. Any such decision can be questioned, and the sub-committee finds itself projected into a discussion of first principles, which are contradictory: then there is a talkative deadlock, until people get tired and go back into the grey area where principles give way to bargaining.

In fact, neither the Personnel Committee nor the Planning Sub-committee have the right to take decisions: they make recommendations to superior bodies, which are charged with the responsibility for the actual decision. One superior body is the Planning Council, which is relatively large and represents many interests. On it there is no gossip about persons and arguments are about principle and policy. There is a degree of formality, which tends to heighten at the time of dispute; there is little sense that power in any form except the crudest—the veto—can be exercised; it is not uncommon to find people putting on an act, sometimes in the form of hinting that although little can be done on this occasion, people should not think that they have heard the last of the matter. Grievances are freely vented and there are not infrequent altercations, but rarely is a recommendation which comes up from the Planning Sub-committee (or from the other subcommittee which serves it) rejected or substantially changed.

The Academic Council, too, is seen as a rubber stamp; posturing is rife; there is a finely sculptured etiquette; and it would be a distinct breach of form to attack a person rather than his performance or the policies for which he stands.

To summarize. When the members of a committee feel that the decisions which they reach will have important practical consequences they tend to seek privacy. This tendency is increased if they also see themselves as a responsible elite or a group of specialists with superior knowledge, cooperating in the interests of the whole. The tendency, conversely, is lessened if decisions are the result of bargaining and compromise between delegates of interest groups which exist outside the committee. There are then two conflicting tendencies. On the one hand there is a temptation to 'go public', particularly on the part of those who are losing the argument; on the other hand, since bargains are reached by compromise, and compromise represents the abandoning of principles, and this in turn might weaken support from outside, even the delegates in an arena committee will be tempted to go in the other direction and to try to keep the bargaining out of sight.

Relative Status and Continuity

If a committee is made up of sets of people who, because of different kinds of expertise or marked differences in status, make noticeably different contributions to the committee's proceedings, then the possibility of developing the kind of morale and mutual confidence which leads in the direction of the private committee is lower than in the case of committees more homogeneously recruited. For example, a major contribution is made to the activities of the Planning Sub-committee (and of the Planning Council) by experts from the Planning Office, who serve as consultants. With such differences around, despite friendships (and enmities) across the boundary, and despite the pervasive use of first names and endless joking, it is very hard for a 'family feeling' to develop. (Indeed, what seems to an outsider a positively Baroque development in wisecracking, may in fact be a symptom of exactly these tensions.) A similar inhibiting effect can be produced by the presence on one committee, where everyone is theoretically equal under the chairman, of senior faculty, junior faculty, and students: it is very hard to prevent hierarchical notions (and resentment against hierarchies) spilling over into the committee. In such committees the members will exhibit a considerable reserve and restraint, a wariness about gossip and a greater concern for their obligations outside the committee than for the committee itself and its tasks. They may not be in a formal sense delegates for outside interest groups, but the fact that these groups or statuses or even levels of expertise exist, has the same effect of pushing the committee towards the public end of the continuum.[7]

There is no such effect on the Personnel Committee. It is true that the members come from different disciplines, but rank differences are not very great or seen as important, and while the difference of discipline means different kinds of knowledge (so that members are not all qualified to the same degree to comment on a particular case) nevertheless all the members make use of essentially the same kind of expertise.[8] There are no members of the Planning staff on the committee, nor do administrators regularly attend as consultants, though occasionally they may be invited to do so. In short, from the point of view of initial homogeneity, the Personnel Committee is ideally suited for the development of a sense of *camaraderie,* a sense of its own collective personality, a readiness to see it stand against the world of outsiders, and an exaggerated sense of its own responsibilities and importance—to become, in a word, the perfectly numinous,[9] perfectly private committee.

The creatures which the Personnel Committee creates to carry out specialized review tasks can turn out to be strikingly different from the parent body. Both the Personnel Committee and its *ad hoc* committees are bound to consider particular cases within the limits imposed on them by university regulations. They see the same file which is submitted by the department, the same collection of evidence about teaching, the same letters from referees testifying to accomplishment in research, the same biography forms which list courses taught, service on committees and publications. Moreover, both the Personnel Committee and its *ad hoc* committee usually have a sense that what they are doing is not trivial. Finally, the *ad hoc* committee should work in total secrecy: no one, other than the members of the Personnel Committee and some administrators, should know who has served on a particular *ad hoc* committee. One might be tempted to conclude from all this that the *ad hoc* committees must, like the Personnel Committee, belong in the category of the private committee. In fact, although secrecy is usually maintained, the *ad hoc* committees are found to conduct themselves with some formality and with the attention to principle and at least the overt avoidance of personal considerations that are characteristic of a public committee.

Why is this so? They operate under highly formalized quasi-judicial procedures, in which the criteria for appointment or advancement are set out, and they are asked to decide whether the candidate meets these criteria. These are just the conditions which enable the parent Personnel Committee to free itself for discussion of persons when selecting the *ad hoc* committee. But the *ad hoc* committee is not expected to gossip about persons. Indeed, the members are selected, as far as possible, with a view to keeping out any personal considerations, friendly or hostile, so that they will have regard only for the rules and for the whole collectivity; so that, in short, they can work as *numen.*[10] An injudicious selection of members can produce bizarre recommendations, which, if followed, would set precedents that would make havoc of the basic rule of bureaucratic equity. Some examples are given elsewhere.

In fact, the Personnel Committee makes free use of gossip and folklore *not* in making its recommendations for appointment or advancement, but only in the selection of members for *ad hoc* committees and, occasionally, in the interpretation of opinions expressed in the file. It is, however, sometimes exceedingly difficult to keep bureaucratic and more personal or political considerations apart, as the following instance demonstrates.

Sometimes scholars offer themselves to universities as teams: old friends; man and wife; or a small team of scientists whose collective research has given them great distinction. In some of these cases, but not in all, the team is a hierarchy, and the university would like to have the leader without having to take on the rest: they want the Superstar and they do not want to pay for the supporting cast. If the Superstar insists, then this condition of appointment is never made a part of the appointment files. It is, as one would expect, something negotiated in the grey area of private bargaining between the chairmen of departments, the deans or other administrators. It is especially tricky if the appointment of the supporting cast is to be made in a department different from that of the Superstar.

There turns out be a neat ranking between the various reviewers in the degrees to which circumstances compel them to see such a situation in all its realistic greyness as distinct from those who are free to close their eyes to bargains and operate entirely by the impersonal rules for measuring the candidate's achievements. At the one end are the chairmen of the departments and the Chancellor or Vice-Chancellor, who must calculate whether there will be a net benefit to the department or the university if one takes on the Superstar at the price of agreeing to the less accomplished cargo which comes along as part of the bargain. (If the cargo is to be placed in a different department, then no doubt that department, usually without its chairman ever having to say so, can expect a future reward for its compliance.)

In fairness, in case you are getting the wrong message from this, one should point out that such decisions are not easy, nor are they, from the standards of the community, in any way immoral; for it is all being done for the good of the group and everyone knows that a blind non-adaptive obedience to the rules can only end in destruction. No leader can remain effective, especially in changing circumstances, if he consistently refuses to retire into the grey area and act in an unprincipled way.

At the other end, the agent least required to use its discretion and most fully gifted with the privilege of merely doing what the rules tell it to do, is the *ad hoc* committee. There is one small item on the front of a personnel file, which indicates relatives employed by the university, but normally it requires much second-guessing to discern that any kind of deal is taking place. When they occasionally pick this up and manage to tune into gossip channels, *ad hoc* committees react in two quite different ways: some of them are annoyed that they have not been taken into confidence and given the 'full information'. ('We are grown up, you know,' one of them said, implying that they knew the way the world 'really' worked.) The other reaction is gratitude that they were protected from being involved in such a messy business and allowed to judge the particular case solely on its own academic merits. Once again, we are in the world of necessary make-believe, the same world in which the judge finds for the plaintiff and then awards him one farthing in damages, thus preserving the rule of law in making a decision in accordance with the law's demands, while allowing for justice and morality through the allocation of penalties.[11] It is indeed a luxury for an advisory committee to keep its hands so clean, from a bureaucratic point of view, while loading the unprincipled decision onto the administrator: without this device the danger of the system dissolving into total chaos would be much greater.

There are other features of the *ad hoc* committees which make it easy for them to be impersonal, guided by principle and bureaucratic. They enjoy complete anonymity, and no one can reproach them for the advice they give. This is less true for the members of the Personnel Committee, for they are distinctly open to pressures conveyed through the informal channels of community living. It is not true at all of the administrator, who makes the final decision, and who can stand by to have the disaffected stamping into his office to express their displeasure in whatever way their mutual personalities and statuses permit.[12] To some extent the *ad hoc* committees have power without responsibility: the result, as in the case of judgement by gossip,[13] of anonymity.

Secondly, these committees meet once to judge a particular case (or sometimes twice or occasionally even three times), but when the case is decided and their advice is given, they are dissolved. Some of the members may know one another off the committee and they may have served before on similar committees, but there is little chance that the members will develop a sense of responsibility and obligation towards one another as persons, or indeed towards others in the chain of reviewers. It is otherwise in the case of the Personnel Committee. When the members are discussing what recommendation to make, not only do they go through the bureaucratic procedure of comparing this case with others (the *ad hoc* committee deals with one case whereas the Personnel Committee might deal with up to thirty in a single week) but they also inevitably make use of another kind of recall: they recall the line of argument taken by their colleagues in other cases and in previous weeks and they know that they will have to meet with these colleagues weekly the rest of the year or longer and they are aware that any decision becomes an accumulation upon their relationship with each other. This is yet more marked when they come to give advice to the Chancellor and his subordinate. They are aware that he sometimes will go into the grey area and strike bargains; they are also aware that they, as advisors, need to maintain his trust and respect, for he is not bound to accept that advice; and they are, inevitably, influenced by the feeling that if they invariably play 'Simon Pure' and give advice exclusively according to the book rather than to the realities of the situation, they will have little influence.

The point is not unfamiliar. Any continuing relationship, either of the members within the committee, knowing that they are going to have to look one another in the eye next week and the week after, or between the committee as a whole and an administrator, will increase the tendency to take into account persons rather than principles.

The labels 'public' and 'private' are in some cases not satisfactory. Under this categorization the *ad hoc* committee is in a strange position. In a quite literal sense it is entirely private, but, for the reasons given (the lack of continuity and continuing obligations) it comes to behave with the impersonality otherwise typical of public committees. The key distinction, once again, seems to be that between community and organization: public meetings involve themselves in matters of policy and principle rather than in gossip about persons and to that extent they are indicative of organizations; the members of an *ad hoc* committee are not given the time and continuity to develop a sense of obligation towards one another, and so, despite the secrecy, they tend to avoid gossip about persons and to remain centered upon principles. Members of the Personnel committee are otherwise: knowing their decisions are likely to be implemented and to have an effect upon themselves and their colleagues, they feel that they must accept responsibility for what they decide: consequently, they take into account the many-sided complexity of a real world of moral persons rather than just being guided by the simple purity of the book of rules.

Conclusion: Community and Organization

Some committees offer the opportunity either to shape or to show off an attitude: their proceedings are marked by ceremonial and formality and posturing to an extent which suggests that the exhibition has an intrinsic value and is not being directed towards getting something done. Along with the ceremonial style goes a concern with policy and principle and a tendency to avoid the discussion of persons.

The committees which show the opposite characteristics, being unceremonious, informal, intolerant of expressive posturing, and ready to talk about persons-in-the-round, have the following features: the members think that what they are doing is of practical (not symbolic) importance; the committee is not large; it has a continuing existence; the members are not delegates from outside interests but answer only to their consciences; their proceedings are private; and the members are relatively homogeneous in status. Attitude-shaping and expressive behavior generally are inappropriate,[14] firstly because the members already know one another's attitudes, and secondly because there is a tacit agreement on values, or (which comes to the same thing) an unquestioning acceptance of the book of rules.

While committees can be found which come near to

exhibiting one or the other extreme, many have mixed characteristics. From examples one begins to get a sense of the relative importance of these different characteristics. For instance, the *ad hoc* committees are small and the members think what they are doing is important; are answerable to their consciences and are guided by what is in the book of rules; are protected by the highest degree of privacy of all the committees considered here; and they are of relatively equal status. But, lacking continuity, the members cannot develop a sense of community among themselves, consequently cannot dispense with some formality in their proceedings and instead, they address themselves in an impersonal way to the maintenance of standards rather than to broader questions of personal and institutional welfare.

There is a further level of enquiry which is made possible because the mix of community and organizational characteristics may vary within one committee at different times. For instance, its heterogeneous membership and its arena-style composition notwithstanding, the Planning subcommittee, after about a year of frustrating conflict, began to develop a sense of community within itself and to take on elite characteristics. This happened despite the fact that it has to cope with questions of policy and that some at least of the members have to go back to their constituencies and give an account of their achievements. (At least the constituents cannot attend the meetings, so there is some degree of secrecy and some latitude for 'laundering' the report.) It seems that this partial privacy, together with a continuing existence and above all a sense that decisions have to be reached and these decisions have important practical consequences are enough to incline this group towards elite behavior. The members develop a sense of community towards one another and begin to feel that they share responsibility for the welfare of the whole institution rather than each one looking after only that segment which he represents.

These are relatively long-term tendencies. One can also look at shifts between the styles of community and organization within a single meeting and at the tactical advantages of bringing about such changes. A discussion of these questions begins in the next chapter.

NOTES

1. 'It is a singular fact, resulting from the structure of Indian institutions, that nearly every transaction, whether social or political, originated or terminated in a council.' (*Morgan* 1962, p. 107) That is how life seems to committee-shy faculty members in some universities: in fact it cannot be so nor could it have been among the Iroquois. Transactions generally originate with individuals and often terminate within the dyad of the originator and his partner, without mediation in the public interest through a committee or a council. The observation, however, suggests that it would be a useful enterprise to identify those features of a transaction which do call for third party intervention.

2. The common way of distinguishing between a committee and a council is to note that the former is responsible to a parent body whereas the latter is sovereign. As usual life is more complicated than this neat legal distinction would suggest. A subordinate advisory committee turns out often to be the one where the decisions are 'really' taken. Conversely, a council which has legal sovereignty makes decisions which affect the lives of others, who may react favorably or unfavorably, and their feedback diminishes *de facto* the council's legally granted sovereignty.

3. One suspects that the tolerance for a woman who turned out to be a ready weeper would not be much greater, and probably no greater in the case of a committee made up of women. This is certainly not to say that sex differences are irrelevant. The stereotypes of the larger society inevitably carry over into committee behavior, and the status of women,

both customary and nowadays legal, affects the process of debate and decision. The influence of external status (although not that of sex) is discussed later in this chapter.

A monograph like this is not a place in which to make systematic cultural comparisons. My interest is in those features (like the contrast between community and organization or between front and back processes in debate and decision) which I would expect to transcend cultural differences: structural similarities encompass different cultural ways of expressing them. In other words, if I am ever fortunate enough to continue this enquiry into universities in—say—India or Latin America, I would expect to be able to ask the same questions about community/organization and public/private decision making, and to find, for example, more emphasis on community in one place and less in another, and different idioms for signalling support for or opposition to the community theme. Another route for making comparisons would be a study of non-academic community/organizations.

Of course, where one culture stops and another begins is a problem more subtle than what would be suggested by a comparison between Eskimos and the Nuer and the rural Welsh. Within a University there are marked cultural differences—different understandings of how the world works and how it should work—between practitioners of the humanities and the natural sciences, between men and women, students and faculty, junior and senior faculty, and so forth. Regretfully I have not had time to pursue these differences.

4. 'Accessible sampling', it should be added quickly, was a joke made in Max Gluckman's seminar composed mainly of former members of the then Rhodes-Livingstone Institute, partly to recognize a real and inescapable difficulty, partly to tease a statistician who attended the discussions.

5. Etiquette, formality, ritual and ceremonial are at the far end of the spectrum of committee features from instrumentality and implementation: they deal with feeling

rather than directly with doing. In this chapter I link etiquette and formal behavior with committee members' culture (ideas of what they are doing) and with variations in status on and off the committee. The function of such behavior is, among other things, that of 'glossing over' differences, concealing hostilities and keeping 'face'. This topic is taken up in chapter 5 and in the conclusion.

6. These terms come from *Bailey*, 1965. At that time I did not perceive the general significance of the contrast between public and private ways of reaching decisions.

7. The reserve, clearly, is a product of mistrust, which itself depends on two conditions: first a belief that a fellow member of the group owes primary allegiance to a set of outsiders different from one's own, and, secondly, that these outsiders are not merely different, but also lack benevolence generally or are allied with one's opponents. The caution is reinforced by 'horror' stories, particularly in those committees, once composed exclusively of faculty, which now have student representatives. Where these are search committees, handling confidential matters, you can always find out (it is said) who is still in the field after yesterday's meeting, by looking at today's edition of the student newspaper. But just the same things are said about exclusively faculty committees: for example, when senior faculty meet to make a recommendation about tenure for a junior colleague (supposed to be confidential at this stage) and those who favor the candidate are outvoted, then, it is said, within an hour one is likely to find a petition in support of the imperilled teacher laid out to be signed by students. Such stories might serve as one indicator of the extent to which elite values prevail in a committee.

8. There is a frequent, and interesting, misunderstanding about the nature of peer review committees: that they are not competent to judge achievement in the many different academic fields over which they have control. What could be more absurd than the chemist and medical man involving themselves in decisions about faculty in the music department

or the history department? There are some natural scientists around still sufficiently Renaissance-minded to consider themselves able to judge any intellectual activity (outside the natural sciences): but even their most naive counterparts in the humanities or the social sciences would draw the line this side of setting themselves up to give a verdict on the state of affairs in high energy physics. The truth is that even within disciplines, it is sometimes hard to find competent referees, particularly when innovation is taking place.

In fact competent scholars are enlisted from outside and the peer review committees do not judge the candidate's research accomplishments, but rather they ask how thoroughly and conscientiously has the review been carried out, what are the sources of bias, have they been controlled, what form of cross-checking has been used, and so forth. Review of a scholar by his peers goes on at two stages: one is opinion on his work of those deemed competent to make the judgement; the second—in which the peer review committees are engaged—is a meta-review, a review of reviews.

Behind this misunderstanding, which is sometimes maintained by a blinkered determination not to see, is the entirely community-like sentiment of discomfort at the notion of counting the achievements of a colleague (or would-be colleague) and thereby making him accountable, an instrument in the service of the organization rather than a person.

9. *Numen* (from which comes the adjective numinous) means first a 'nod'; then it comes to mean 'command, will, authority'; then 'divine will, supreme authority, divine majesty'. I have extended this (*Bailey*, 1972) to mean the person or the institution which claims the legitimate right to stand for the collectivity and to represent a principle of orderliness, a sacred body which by definition has no self-interest apart from the general interest, answerable to no one since it is itself God, or at least his voice.

10. See note 9 of this chapter.

11. See *Van Velsen*, p. 148.

12. *Kerr*, p. 40 '. . . but the greatest of these is fortitude since others have so little charity.' Administrators lack the protection of anonymity. See note 8 of chapter 3.

13. See chapter 5.

14. Of course there is no committee entirely free from attitude-shaping. Committees work through debate and part of every debate is an attempt to change values and assumptions. But in private committees the process is more subtle and more delicate; the whole person has to be shaped, something more than just the exposure of an attitude to the heat of an ideology which will cause it to take on the right form; the process takes time and there is likely to be a 'shaking down' period before members discover that they have a tacit agreement on values and now only rarely need to remind each other what these values are.

CHAPTER FIVE

Arenas and Enmities

Four Arenas

'Arena' here refers to those myths which people have about how decisions are taken, for example, to allocate such scarce resources as new faculty positions, funds for graduate students and teaching assistants, money to buy equipment for instruction and research, and so forth.

There are four myths about how such allocations are made: through rational bureaucratic procedures and formulae directed towards the interests of the collectivity; through competition between strong men (baronial politics); through a conflict between central administrators and the strong men banded together (the politics of Runnymede); and finally, by a patronage network operating—in some universities, but not in all—off-stage and out of the back door.

These four myths each suggest that different strategies will be appropriate. If you believe that all the necessary wisdom is already contained in the Manuals of Procedure, you need to know what is in those manuals and be able to quote them on the appropriate occasions: a tactic which can be devastatingly effective. If you believe that you are working in a rational bureaucracy, then it pays to be able to wax eloquent about goals and to argue rationally about the means to reach those goals. If you are competitive then the first priority must be to cultivate a reputation for being a formidable person. Finally, if you believe that patronage dispenses most of the desirable resources within the university, then the cultivation of appropriate personal relationships is more important than knowing the rule book or having forensic skills or a muscular personality.

Of the several dimensions which distinguish these four arena myths, I deal with only two. One concerns strategies; what conditions decide when it is appropriate to use a public strategy and when going through the back door pays off better. The second question, which is connected but not identical, is one of the many transformations of the distinction between 'community' and 'organization': to what degree does each myth see persons in an instrumental fashion (as does the myth of rational bureaucracy) rather than as rounded human beings, as do the others. The second question is the more fundamental, since from the perception of the nature of the arena, the appropriateness of strategies is decided.

I shall consider two main sets of contextual variables: the actors and the topic. By finding the appropriate dimensions along which to compare types of actor and types of topic we can begin to predict degrees of personalization and degrees of openness in the arena.

Actors and Reputations

Certain performances, both in universities and elsewhere, are easy to describe but difficult to explain. To some extent performances are the product of physiological and psychological conditions which I take as given. Other factors, accounting for how a man chooses to look at his world, are more accessible: the kind of networks into which he is tied; the length of time for which he has served the institution; the degree of success which he sees himself as having had in his career; all these will help decide whether he chooses to operate in public or in private, to attempt to apply the leverage of rules and principles rather than to exploit personal connections.

Other things being equal—in this case a large category—as the young university person gets to be an old university person, he will learn to see persons as dominant over rules and the private networks or patronage as more comfortable and more productive than public politicking. It is a very simple proposition: that the longer you live in a community, other things being equal, the more likely you are to know how to make it respond to your wishes with the least possible cost. The same process, of course, can also teach you to limit your wishes according to what you have learned is available.

In the institutions of learning which I have attended, ranging from one which was found in the year AD 1340 to others which were founded less than a decade ago, there have always been elder statesmen or founding fathers; men with great personal credibility which was maintained often because it was never challenged for they were seldom if ever required to defend their point of view in public; cronies of one another; the advisors of those in power, and having the ultimate privilege of the elder in any community, power without being held publicly accountable for it. In a word, they are the charter members of the community. They sit on the right hand of the king and they are his courtiers. They may or may not also hold public office or enter into public debate, but the point is that given certain other characteristics, survival alone with a moderate degree of success can enhance a man's reputation sufficiently to make it unnecessary for him to practice any style of politics except that of the courtier.[1] Indeed, the term 'courtier', suggesting nowadays the privileged sycophant, idle and snug at the public expense, may be inappropriate: they have privilege in plenty but in their own eyes and in those of the king, they earn it because they are the first to whom he turns for disinterested and sound advice.

Such men see the courtly side of politics in a manner which Parsons calls 'fiduciary':[2] that is, they are guardians of the sacra of the community, the embodiment, so to speak, of *numen.*[3] They are the 'elders', and are to be contrasted with another set of people who believe in the myth of a courtly style of politics, but see it as a way of obtaining resources rather than as a set of obligations. For the elder statesman service as a courtier is its own intrinsic reward: for others such service is directed towards maximizing some other kind of reward. As one of Adrian Mayer's politicians put it, 'They are on the lookout for which vein will bleed the most';[4] wholly cynical and following that style of politics as long as it pays them to do so: they are would-be 'big men'.[5]

Those are the people who work for preference behind the scenes. One's ability to do so improves with familiarity. The mode of action in both cases is private: but for the elder the end is the public goal of the maintenance of tradition. (Of course you can flip the coin back again and present the counter-myth that they are interested in tradition because through it alone they can maintain power.)

Every organization and every community will also contain people who believe that the right kind of political competition is that which is conducted in the open. Again, it seems unlikely to me that there will be just one kind of person acting in this way. There are soap-box people. But there are also essentially shy men, who have systematic minds, believe in the rules and subscribe to the doctrine of rational solutions, and whose actions are public to the extent that they are justified by rules of procedures and of substance,which in turn derive their legitimacy from the very fact of being public. In many countries the civil servant works behind a screen of anonymity, but what he does and above all the reason why he does it has to be public: that is, accessible to a public which has the right to demand the information.

There is a second sense of 'public politics' familiar in the distinction between the politician and the civil servant. The politician puts himself across to an audience, seeking to establish charisma, trying to have himself accepted as a person-in-the-round while, paradoxically, dealing in the fashion of mass-production with the many. The operation is essentially a confidence trick by which the many are persuaded to accord the trust and confidence found in a moral relationship, while receiving in return a mere simulacrum, which pretends to morality but in fact is instrumental. These are the men who can impress the multitude and that style of politics is not available to someone who does not have those peculiar talents.

To summarize: to adopt one or another or some combination of the arena myths, and to use the appropriate strategies, certain qualifications are required. If you invariably make a mess of personal relationships and invariably mismanage face-to-face encounters, then you will learn to stay away from courtly politics. Conversely, if you are utterly without public charm or at least a heavy presence, there is no place for you in baronial politics or the politics of Runnymede. It seems to follow that if you have neither private nor public charm, then the best way out is to become a rational bureaucrat.

Something should be said about failures, for people are sometimes slow to learn from experience, and cling to one or another myth although continually failing to get what they appear to want. For example, the court politician who has not learned the art of knowing what can be safely leaked to whom and what cannot, does not last long. I know of one man, nominated for an executive position, who knocked himself through the ropes before he even started by announcing who was on his enemies' list and would therefore be harassed as soon as he got into a position of power: he never did.

More interesting, because on top of stupidity is added a form of sacrifice, are those not uncommon persons who may be good speakers and who might display a degree of charisma, if they were not invariably champions of lost causes. A Berhampur newspaper commemorating the birth-anniversary of an Indian Freedom Fighter, dead some years, whose career had gone from one disastrous act of protest to another, wrote; 'At least he should be praised and remembered for his revolting character.' You can see what the editorial meant. There are some university politicians out of the same mold: they may be true believers in a lost cause; or they may defend the indefensible because they like being knocked down. Their actions are public and open and part of the rather impersonal democracy by which we are supposed to govern ourselves. Their reception, however, is entirely characteristic of the community: they are tolerated with amusement or mild scorn; their support is feared and enmity is welcomed: they are the bane of the senate and care is taken to keep them out of positions of responsibility and off committees which have work to do because their presence is always non-productive and sometimes disruptive.

In short, these are the kinds of personal histories which make for the adoption of one or another myth of political interaction: that it is and should be mainly mainly a public affair as against the belief that the most effective things are done behind closed doors; secondly that a political system is a set of rules to be followed rather than a set of persons to be manipulated. Now let us consider how these variables are influenced by the topic or the issue.

Policies and Scandals

Certain topics and certain issues call for open discussion: others incline towards the politics of confidentiality (what goes on behind the scenes and behind the hand).

Some public discussions are ritualized affirmations of well-known and broadly accepted policies: we are against sin or in favor of motherhood. They are essentially expressive occasions rather than a forum for deciding policy. Some committees exist only so that attitudes and opinions may be expressed and reinforced.

Sometimes genuine controversy erupts in these committees, and when this happens most of those present experience discomfort, because they have become accustomed to the ceremonial expressions of solidarity which are normal on those occasions. It follows that those who stage-manage such meetings are usually careful to keep off the agenda and out of discussion topics which are genuinely divisive. Thus, when University Hall or rival universities are blasted, the atmosphere is one of contented indignation: things are normal. But when, on another occasion, someone asserts that a scandalously large amount of time is devoted to research and a scandalously small amount of time to teaching, people get a sense of the boat being rocked and calmness returns only when the chairman takes the matter out of discussion by some suggestion like 'Why don't you and I and Ben get together later this week and get this thing sorted out and then we can report back . . .'

Secondly, there are some topics which may be controversial but which must receive public discussion partly because the rules say that they must and partly because any decision has to be accepted and understood and implemented by a relatively large number of people. Thus curriculum matters, a proposal to abolish grades, to institute some compulsory course in science for students of the humanities, or in the humanities for science students, and so forth, is argued about in public and often decided by a vote. It is always possible that a few people are powerful enough to take the decision and then have it ratified by the public assembly, but without the ratification the decision is not valid and those who do not like it may be able to ignore it.

In short, views are openly aired when they are non-controversial, when the rules require that they be aired (whether controversial or not), and when they cannot be implemented unless there is a wide degree of understanding and agreement.

At the opposite extreme is the scandal. Scandals in a community are matters about which everyone gets to know but no one can use openly as a basis for action or for shaping attitudes. The reason is that, by its very nature, such talk would be excessively destructive. If the dean of the men's college is having an affair with the dean of the lady's college—or worse the dean of another men's college—then that issue is unlikely to surface in so many words on the senate floor. Secondly, just as there is a concern for the well-being of the community as a whole, so also there is a concern for its members. If something has to be done about the colleague who is having trouble with the bottle or with the marital partner, because the trouble is getting in the way of his or her performance in the university, it is generally agreed that this is something to be done in private and should not be the object of a public judicial procedure. To open the box is to risk losing support. Of course, there are limits: certain actions may be so scandalous that they must become the object of open legal sanctioning procedures: to hush the thing up would be too great a cost not only in terms of justice but also for the self-respect of the community. But it remains an interesting thought that you are likely to be less punished for stealing a colleague's wife or husband than for stealing and publishing his or her ideas.

Thus we have two extreme cases: topics which demand to be aired in the open and others which, like breaking wind, are a source of embarrassment on public occasions.

But, as ever, extreme cases are the simple cases and certainly less challenging to the analyst than are the intermediate. To make this clear, I will describe a set of events which I have put together from several different sources, including some fiction. It continues our exploration of the dimensions of public and private, and of person and system, in the context of a subject of concern to Lewis Henry Morgan: controlling executive authorities through popular or representative assemblies.

Going Public

There are four characters in this play. First is the Chairman who initiates a file requesting that the second character, the Candidate, should be appointed to a senior professorial post. Decisions in such cases are made by the third character, the President, but he is obliged to listen to the advice of the various faculty reviewers who can be summarized in the fourth character, the Objector.

To understand the play you need to remember the myths which faculty have about administration, and administration about faculty, and you need also to recall the strange mixture of contempt and apprehension which scholars seem to feel for those of their number who are conspicuously successful in manipulating the outside world. The Candidate, indeed, would probably not have been generally judged a 'popularizer' (the whole affair took place behind the screen of confidentiality and was never opened to the general university public) but he would have been judged a 'hustler'.[6] He had been unusually successful in extracting grants from public sources, in stage-managing conferences, in advising government agencies and of his long, and at first sight, impressive list of publications, more than a few were inaccessible to reviewers because they were secret reports to government or commercial agencies and many of the rest were edited reports of conferences and workshops. In the eyes of reviewers, this fine record of public service and successful manipulation of research agencies and institutions did not make up for the absence of any distinguished contribution, by the person himself, to his subject. This evaluation was strengthened by a similar opinion from outside referees and it was acknowledged, somewhat reluctantly, by the Chairman and his colleagues.

These same qualities commended the Candidate both to the Chairman and to the President. Granted that the Candidate's arrival would not enhance the reputation of the department in the eyes of other scholars, he came nevertheless from a distinguished university and he had many counter-balancing qualities such as a reputation for energy and getting things done, not to mention an extensive and effect network which could be used to bring funds to the department.

The battle began with the President and Chairman on one side in opposition to the reviewers, represented by the Objector. Even leaving out of consideration the merits and demerits of the Candidate, this alignment is predictable. The President, one suspects, like many other Presidents saw himself and his departmental chairmen in the fashion of Napoleon and his generals: accountable only to themselves and to the goals which they had set. Secondly, no Chairman would be human if he did not resent outsiders telling him what he could or could not do within his own department.

An occasion like this could generate much rhetoric, since it involves some of the fundamental and contradictory myths of the academy. The Objector, for example, might have argued in a distinctly numinous way, that he was the trustee for scholarly excellence: furthermore, the future of academic self-government was in his hands, for to give way to the two representatives of the executive powers would substantially weaken future popular control over them. From the other side it might have been argued that second-guessing the judgement of the Chairman and the President was an insult to the competence of the former and the trustworthiness of the latter. Furthermore, to insist on the criterion scholarship alone, would be to stifle any innovation and any chance of adapting the institution to the world around it, and without such adaptation the institution would be destroyed.

But, in fact, in my play, when the argument is finally joined, much of it is conducted on an altogether less exalted level. We join the play after the Chairman has renewed his appeal to the President and the latter has summoned the Objector so that they may discuss the case.

The exchange was at first conducted largely in normative

terms. Both agreed that no one should be appointed who did not reach the high standards of scholarship required at that university. The President eventually conceded that the Candidate might not quite reach these standards—and the President was somewhat deflated when he realized that the Chairman agreed with this judgement—but argued the need for innovation and the Candidate's proven ability to raise money. .The Objector replied that a more thorough search would no doubt find someone who was both a good scholar and able to carry out the entrepreneurial tasks. Innovation need not be bought at the price of hiring indifferent scholars: indeed—and here the argument sank to a less impersonal level—there were several disastrous appointments made on exactly this principle still with us to give warning not to do so again.

But this exchange, although it was the one through which the President formally decided to change sides and deny the appointment, was, at least in my play, just the tip of an iceberg of less explicit communication.

Firstly, for reasons that will be apparent shortly, the Objector set out to show that he and the other reviewers on this occasion 'meant business'. Besides the use of such phrases as 'deep concern', he allowed a touch of anger and emotion to show, and he distanced himself by refusing refreshments and abstaining from the customary first name in favor of the title. Such behavior in fact carries two messages: one, already mentioned, is that people who feel deeply are also likely to act strongly—even at their own cost; secondly, it lessens the temptation for the President to try seduction by making clear that maintaining the rules and the system is more important than keeping friendships.

Apart from this symbolic interaction, there may have been a whole other play going on behind the scene. This play is called 'Going Public'. The reviewers, when they heard that their original advice might be disregarded, had discussed this possibility, but had considerable trouble working out what, in terms of concrete action, it could mean.

The whole episode, the contents of the file, the name of the Candidate, of the department, of most reviewers and all the referees, constitute restricted information. Only the reviewers and the President and some of his staff have the right to see the documents after they leave the department: letters are solicited from referees with the understanding that they will be confidential; and it is altogether impossible to 'go public' in any literal sense without violating some important rules and so losing the support of many people who might otherwise have been favorable.

There is, in fact, only one way known to me to 'go public'—at least in an open way and not through 'leaks'—on such occasions: this is resignation. The committee or its chairman must announce that they are unwilling to continue advising the President, because their advice has been unjustly disregarded. The resignation would in fact be an advertisement to a larger audience that his people no longer have confidence in their President.

There are two separate considerations in this. Firstly, even those who see a university as a section in a larger state bureaucracy, paradoxically expect it to be self-contained in certain respects. The leader of any section should be able to settle internal disputes without allowing them to rise higher in the machine. This is the familiar cautionary tale of the Collector in India whose career is forever blighted because he once had to call in the military to restore order in his District. Metaphors like 'can't run his own ship' are heard. Consequently, no administrator with ambitions likes to allow dissension between his subordinates (in this case the Chairman and the Objector) to reach the point at which one of them, or both of them, appeal to an official superior to him or to a wider public.

The second point to be illustrated by our play is that when the Objector decides to put pressure on the President, he has at his disposal only the most limited of sanctions, limited because they are also the most extreme. It is like being outcasted in India: a gigantic penalty applied only in extreme cases. It is also like the threat of nuclear war: a horrendous sanction, the very enormity of which is a deterrent just because the cost of using the ultimate weapon is so great and because the user too will very likely be destroyed. This ultimate weapon, for advisers who have moral but not legal sanctions at their disposal, is an act of resignation, stage-managed with some publicity.

The costs are high. Once you resign, you have fired off your rockets and you have no more weapons. You have put yourself out of the battle, sacrificed yourself, except in those rare circumstances in which your support is so strong and your stand so righteous that the administrator will be forced to ask you back. Moreover, too frequently used, the threat of resignation becomes a blot on the career like the administrator's failure to solve problems within his own section. You acquire a reputation for being unstable and unreliable, incapable of seeing a job through to the end, and so forth.

In short, to go public in these circumstances is to cross the Rubicon, to burn the boats, to lash the wheel on a collision course: in fact to deny the possibility of compromise and make sure that the outcome will be victory for one side and for the other defeat. To go public may be to do something which in the myth of a community is wholly inappropriate—to risk the destruction of the community.

Even an open threat to go public can itself have a disruptive effect, for Presidents and other executive people keep a watchful eye on their own reputation for firmness, and that kind of publicity puts the reputation at risk. For this reason it pays the Objector to flatter a little and to try to convince the President it is in his own best interest and in the best interest of the institution to follow the Objector's advice. If there is to be a threat of resignation, it has to be done in such a way that the President can pretend he knows nothing about it and that it did not influence his decision. Universities turn out to be such a convenient blend of organization and community that there is no difficulty in letting it be known to one or two key persons, in confidence of course, that the wrong decision will mean resignation: the President will certainly be able to build that knowledge into his calculations without having formally to countenance it.

There remains one final act. In it the President makes arrangements so that the Objector and other reviewers may meet the Chairman and have a general discussion about the department's recruitment policy in the future. The meeting is a small, informal affair and no one except the President and those who attended knows that it took place.

In all this appears a precept: the maintenance of public normative standards, such as a high quality faculty and democratic procedures in the university must be so managed as to do the least possible damage to continued relatively harmonious, or apparently harmonious, community relationships.

Let us look at how the four actors stood at the end of the play. The President has been able to reverse an earlier decision without having to appear either foolish or lacking in firmness. Any threats or comments which might have damaged him were made in such a way that he could claim not to have heard them and to have acted purely in the best interests of the institution.

The Objector also comes out reasonably well. He has succeeded in protecting the two citadels of academic standards and academic democracy: and he has done so without having to use the ultimate weapon and so disqualify himself from the game in the future.

The Chairman, apparently, is the loser, having been unable to preserve his department from outside interference. But notice that steps are taken to prevent, or try to prevent this from being only the first of several such episodes. A heavy injection of person-to-person contact should make it harder for both sides to stand on principle in the future,[7] and make it easier for them to negotiate a settlement in private before they have committed themselves to positions from which they cannot withdraw without loss of face.

Finally, there is the Candidate. Poor man: once deemed unfit by reviewers to join their community of scholars, he has become nothing more than an instrument, condemned solely on his academic record and ignored as a person. All the participants, especially the President and the Objector, make sure that, if there are costs to be paid for the maintenance of academic standards and academic democracy, these costs shall, if possible, fall on someone outside the community.

What does this episode signify?

There are choices: people dispute about goals and for such disputes there can be no reasoned outcome. People recognize four kinds of arena in which disputes can take place: the rational bureaucracy, the baronial contest, Runnymede, and the politics of the king's court. These differ along the two dimensions of personal/impersonal relationships and open/covert strategies. Speaking roughly a man's choice of strategy and his selection of the relevant arena will depend firstly on his personality; secondly on his network connections and the time he has lived in the community; and thirdly, on the nature of the topic under dispute, whether it is noncontroversial, controversial but of necessity public, or, thirdly, excessively disruptive of community feeling.

But the episode goes beyond the reach of this conceptual framework. Identifying the four arenas and the dimensions which discriminate between them are acts of analytic simplification: the move upwards is in the direction of simplicity. But the move downwards from the repertoire to the performance is away from simplicity towards subtlety. The nearer one comes to action and implementation, the more delicate must be the mix between front and back strategies, and the more fragile becomes the apparatus for communication. The coarse moves are those which are made in public.

The next section, on enmity and its control, examines further the delicate pretence by means of which conflict is kept short of the point of chaos.

Enmity

When people quarrel about fundamental goals and continue to hold contradictory first principles, there is no reasoned way of resolving the dispute. Nevertheless, in the arguments described earlier, there are features which certainly deserve the adjective 'rational'. The contests are about the distribution of resources, or the application of one or another rule to a given situation, and the debate is regarded by each of the competitors as a means towards an end: the contest itself has no intrinsic value. Indeed, the reverse is true: whatever the real feelings, it is customary at least in universities to enter into disputes with a note of regret that the problem could not have been solved in other and less contentious ways.

Such forms of contending are characteristic of organizations and bureaucracies. Members are bound by rules, limiting the strategies they may employ and the resources which they are allowed to bring to the field of contest. They are expected to be aware of a 'reality' which constrains their activities; they are expected to have relatively clearly enunciated final goals which make compromise easier, because they are also shared goals; and, above all, they are expected to behave in an impersonal fashion, using only that part of themselves which is the bureaucratic mind and closing off all emotions.

There is another type of contest. To belong to a community is to treat others and to be treated by them as a complete human being, to be given moral status. This is exactly what is not done in the 'rational' contests described above, for in them the contestants are required to ignore the many-sidedness of themselves and of other persons.

Membership in a moral community can be warm and supportive; being given tenure one is accepted into the group in return for qualities rather than as a reward for specific performances. One belongs as to a family: but remember that quite a large proportion of murders are within families and few of those are done to collect an insurance or to speed up an inheritance. Whether carefully planned or executed on an impulse, they occur because the victim has become in the eyes of the killer a different person, his failings being so continuous or on a particular occasion so spectacular that he has become 'a bad lot'. In short, not only a family but any moral community contains relationships of enmity, as well as those of amity, and the former are as much a part of the fabric of a community as are the latter.

Such enmity is 'mindless' or 'irrational'. These adjectives do not mean that the feelings cannot be rationally explained as the product of unconscious forces, but rather that, when challenged to explain his hostility, a man will either produce no reason at all, or produce some cause that is so manifestly inadequate to account for the strength of his hostility, that others will say, 'But that is quite out of proportion!' or, more directly, 'You must be mad!' Secondly, when seeking to account for his feelings, a man will rather quickly move away from what the hated person has done, or even from 'what he stands for' to a claim that he is essentially an evil person.

Such hostility is brought under control by other members of the community in two ways. Firstly 'personalized' statements of hostility made in public are severely discouraged, and driven underground where, in the form of gossip, the explosions are muffled and less damaging. Secondly, efforts are made to find some 'proper' reasons for the hostility, to make the embittered person acknowledge these, and then demonstrate that they are not enough to justify the strength of his feelings, and that he can achieve whatever end he has in mind without forcing a combat.

Indication of Enmity

Occasionally one encounters behavior distressingly out of line with what one would like to think is the general tenor of the Academy. Many years ago a chairman fell seriously ill. I chanced to meet a senior member of his department and enquired after the sick man. The reply startled me. In a tone of voice and in a manner that ruled out joking, he said, 'He hasn't died yet. I hope he does.' I was no more than an acquaintance, both of the sick man and of the man who wished him dead, and I did not know nor did I ever find out what had gone on between them to produce such bitter animosity. Many years later I still find it hard to imagine that offenses in the normal run of what goes on in departments could have been so heinous as to make this hatred understandable and dispel my feeling that there was something odd about a man who would make a remark like that to a mere acquaintance.

Two features in this story stand out. Firstly the extremity and the violence of the statement indicate that, although the dislike may have begun because of what the sick man had done, perhaps in the course of 'rational' competition of the kind described earlier, the judgement no longer concerned what he did, but rather what he was. The hostility was not a product (or not only or no longer a product) of some structured opposition between chairman and subordinate but was directed at the person for what he was, and no longer for what he did in the performance of a role. In brief, the hostility had become, at least so far as that person was concerned, an end in itself, and one suspects that if reasons were given for the dislike, they would turn out to be mere rationalizations.[8]

The second feature in this small incident is that the remark was not made to a crony or a confidant who could expect to be entrusted with unkind judgements and malicious information.

Delivered to me, a comparative stranger, the message not only said that the man wished his chairman dead, but also he didn't care who knew it. Once again we are noticing the front stage, on which normally principles are displayed and proclaimed: on this occasion the display was one of mindless hatred.

My next example is in the realm of comedy. When putting together *ad hoc* committees to advise about hiring, firing and promoting faculty, there are various regulations which govern the selection of persons and there are further 'folk' rules which help to shut off the effect of personal animosities, to prevent needless altercations, and to make sure that the committee can go about its task as far as possible, in a rational fashion. Occasionally, mistakes are made and the committee becomes a bear pit in which old grudges are dusted off and given an airing, animosities hitherto unknown come to light, and, in extreme cases, the committee falls apart without ever producing a report, or (in one instance) five members produced five conflicting reports (all naturally in a minority) or, at best, the report has relatively little to do with the task set and is nothing but an indirect history of resurrected antipathies.

These unfortunate occurrences are themselves indications of mindless hostility and they illustrate another of its features. Implicit in my description is a judgement (which is not only mine but that of academics in general) that such personal animosities are destructive and deplorable. While 'rational' competition can be seen as a means towards some agreed end, a way of reaching a decision, animosities which are directed at the person have, according to the myth, no useful product. It may do the person good to let off steam, but it disrupts the harmonious working of the community. Furthermore, if you define the university as an organization, then the personal animosities are irrational because they stand in the way of the organization's goals.

Occasionally, when people are asked to serve on *ad hoc* committees, they manage to find out before the committee meets who will be their colleagues. It is not unknown for someone to take the wholly rational step of refusing to serve, and letting it be known that he has done so because he cannot stand the sight of someone else who will be on that committee. On one occasion we learned the reason (if you can call it that) for the enmity: the two men were antagonists in the arena of Little League Baseball. Other things, evidently, besides baseball for young people deserve the adjective 'little'.

This incident will serve to point up some of the features already attributed by the myth to mindless hostility and to illustrate one other, which is the pervasive capacity of such feelings of enmity. They cross boundaries and the hostility displayed in one field will surely surface in other fields, even across such unlikely boundaries as that between the university senate and children playing baseball. This, I suppose, is another reason for calling such animosities 'fundamental': they erase the reasoned segmentation and hierarchies of an ordered life.

Finally notice that these antipathies are often about issues which to other people seem trivialities. How can two adult men, of high intelligence and otherwise much respected, find themselves unable to cooperate in conducting important affairs for the institution to which they belong, because of something so essentially unimportant as children's games? Surely there must be some 'real' reasons behind this feeble rationalization? The myth is of little help, for it delights in pointing out that fundamental enmities often arise from the slightest causes and, in effect, it offers as an explanation nothing but that old Yorkshire saying 'There's nowt so queer as folk'.

To summarize. Mindless hostility was contrasted with the rational process of debate or competition in which the competitors have an extrinsic goal in mind: discovering the truth, making a compromise, or in some other way reaching a decision. As Coser and others have pointed out, if they chance upon a better way of attaining this goal than by competing with one another, they will drop the competition. But mindless hostility is an end in itself. While rational competition moves towards the resolution of the point at issue and therefore towards its own liquidation, mindless hostility goes in the opposite direction, not only sustaining but also magnifying itself.

Secondly, mindless hostility is to be contrasted with the sentiment of amity and mutual regard, thought to be proper in a community. Animosity is deplored because those whom others consider to be in one community and are therefore expected to grant each other status as full human beings, instead deny one another's fitness to belong to the community.

Thus, both from the point of view of the university as a community and as an organization, the display of mindless hostility is deplorable; in the first case it breaks the cardinal rule of mutual trust and consideration, and in the second case it imports judgements of person, which are improper in an organization and pervert the rational competitive process of purposeful debate into an irrational and unproductive expression of personal hostility. Since from both points of view the behavior is deplorable, we should not be surprised to find that a part of the myth of mindless hostility between university colleagues is made up of customs which serve to keep the hostility under control. The two remaining aspects of the cases described above turn out to be a part of this process of control: firstly it seems to be obligatory to deny that the hostility is in fact mindless by producing reasons (even if trivial) to account for such feelings. Mindless hostility has to be expressed in the form of one of its opposites: rationality. Secondly, mindless hostility, if it is not cloaked in a rational form, should not be openly expressed but must be transmitted through channels of gossip and rumor. Its open expression is deplored, for such behavior is an irrelevant waste of time in an organization, and a sin in a community.

Controls over Enmity

In looking at particular cases, there is no point in asking whether an offensive action was in fact justified and rational or whether it arose really from some mindless antagonism. Our interest rather is in claims and assertions: in the way in which these contrasting labels can be used to control and educate persons and so prevent the community or the organization from being damaged through the expression of internal animosities.

Within a community there is a rule that ranks should be closed against outsiders: it is wrong to reveal internal dissensions to outsiders, and it is especially wrong to use contacts with outsiders in order to damage a fellow member of the community. I shall illustrate this through two instances, both of which concern an experimental School of Education, part of a university but privileged to receive special funds from the Ministry in order to carry out its program. From the point of view of many of the faculty, who were expected to lend a hand in the operations of the School, the somewhat bizarre curriculum and the unfamiliar methods of recruiting students made the enterprise suspect. Some departments cooperated more than others with the new School: a few developed a quite resolute hostility towards it.

One of these departments, not known for its friendliness towards the new School, was receiving a visitation from a grant-giving body. The visitors interviewed, among many others, a decanal committee on which sat the Head of the new School, along with deans and sub-vice-chancellors. One by one they gave their opinion of the department, praise being heaped upon praise, until it came to the turn of the Head of the new School. He said that the department was obstructive, old-fashioned, lacking in a spirit of innovation and altogether unworthy of support. The visitation committee, perhaps because such sentiments made a change, and perhaps because they were short of money anyway, egged him on and gave no one else on that committee a chance to undo the damage.

Within minutes of the end of that meeting, five of those present had telephoned the chairman of the department to tell him of these disastrous happenings, and to assure him that they would make clear their displeasure to the Head of the new School and make him understand that further behavior of this kind would make life difficult for him in the future. Whether they did any of this is not known.

The department, which did not get its grant, united in condemning the Head's action as an act of malice and nothing more. In his own defense, he said that he was not aware of any feelings of hostility towards the department, but had simply answered truthfully the questions that were asked of him. The department replied that he was mistaken, but in any case truth was not the issue. He had failed to live up to his obligations to the community.

They reminded him of another incident which had taken place only a short time before. This time the School of Education was under the spotlight. During its first years, putting into practice unfamiliar ideas by recruiting strange faculty and a curious assortment of students, it had become an institution of some notoriety, the object of not infrequent newspaper articles alleging scandal and mismanagement. The issue became large enough for the Ministry to appoint a committee of enquiry, which came down to the university and, among others, questioned all the departmental chairmen about the School. It so happened that the first man questioned was implacably hostile towards the School, so much so that he had taken the trouble to draw up a formidable list of accusations and evidence to back them. As each succeeding chairman came into the room, the committee of enquiry produced some of these accusations, saying from where they had come and asking for comments. Every chairman gave the committee the same message: they should not take the accuser too seriously, for, although brilliant in his subject and in his teaching and in that respect a great asset to the university, he was also known to be a little crazy, and not too much notice should be taken of what he said. The truth, they asserted, was that the School, although like any other new institution having some teething difficulties, was in fact a sound and promising venture, innovative certainly but academically entirely respectable. Most of those who took this line were consciously covering up a bad situation, because they saw it as *their* situation and because their colleagues would suffer if they did not. Whether the first man's accusations were true or not, evidently they believed he was quite wrong to let his hostility lead him into making damaging accusations in front of outsiders.

In both cases, the effect was to write off as an irrelevance the reason given by the two objectors (that they were telling the truth). They had allowed personal dislikes to spill over into arenas, where it was not proper for them to be exercised. To do so was an indication of irrationality and a betrayal of the community.

The third instance is more subtle and in it the controls were such that the open accusation which might have endangered community relations were never quite made. It concerns an institution, mostly engaged in research, partly funded by money from the Ministry via the university to which it was attached, and partly by research grants from industry and from other government sources than the Ministry of Education. Some of those in the Institute, in the intervals of contract work and consulting overseas, diverted themselves by teaching courses in the university. Not many of them did this, but those who did stayed at the task and the courses were well received.

We now move to a Planning Committee discussing the allocation of new teaching positions and in particular a proposal that one of these lectureships should be given to the Institute to help maintain the courses which it taught in the university. One of those present thereupon proposed that the Director of the Research Institute should be required to guarantee in writing that in return for the teaching post he would see that the course continued in being. (The Director was not present at the meeting.)

Someone else said, 'One does not do that sort of thing' a turn of phrase which in England certainly indicates that community norms are being invoked. It was quite unnecessary for the speaker to spell out what sort of thing it was one did not do, and why it should not be done, and he said no more. But the other man persisted and the level of embarrassment rose until the vice-chancellor, wise as Solon said, 'I will write him a letter and I will ask him to make sure that the course continues because it is so well received by the students and others.' Notice the obliqueness: there is no mention of the implied contract: on the surface nothing more than a fraternal expression of gratitude and esteem, coupled with a request.

It should have silenced the objector, but he went on saying that he thought it would be a mistake not to get a written guarantee from the Director. Then people said that a letter of that kind from the vice-chancellor provided the best possible guarantee, for it was inconceivable that the Director would disregard the request in it: in fact, as everyone knew, it was quite conceivable.

People thought that the objector had behaved in this way because he disliked heartily the Director. But he could not voice this dislike: he could not even use the word 'untrustworthy': instead he asked for a *written* guarantee, thus getting the substance of his dislike across but at the same time leaving himself open a retreat into bureaucratic considerations about change of personnel, the need for records and so forth. Once he was compelled to cloak the dislike by giving a reason for his proposal, discussion could then proceed along ostensibly reasonable lines to achieve the end which he had described (ensuring that the course would continue) while at the same time making sure that the occasion could not be used by him to work off his antipathies. Throughout the discussion no one openly referred to the objector's animosities, or to the risk that the Director might take offense if such a letter as the objector wished came to be written. Such personal considerations were known to all those present, but carefully concealed beneath a flow of loquacious rationality.

Indeed, one does not need incidents of this kind to understand what I am saying. Any community remains in operation through the maintenance of such 'basic lies' as that its members are not moved by hostility towards one another. Some time ago I attended a brief course in which all those in managerial and administrative positions in the university, together with a few outsiders, were given elementary instruction in better management. We played various games in order to prove to ourselves that people in organizations were more contented if they had a sense of being consulted in taking important decisions. One exercise recommended was called 'planned renegotiation'. In brief, this meant that if you felt yourself getting sore at what someone else was doing, you should not let your animosity pile up to the point where the only outcome would be a row, but you should go to him and bring things out into the open and renegotiate positions to your mutual satisfaction. At first sight this is attractive: on further thought it is not, for I can think of no swifter way of upsetting someone else than by going in at frequent intervals and telling him that he is upsetting you or asking him why he is upset with you. More generally, at least some 'planned renegotiations' must fail, because the notion assumes an ultimate congruence of values. We are back at the same point of saying that the only way to deal with some troubles is by pretending that they are not there: hearts on the sleeves may be less appropriate than a nice combination of reserve and hypocrisy.[9]

In brief, I am arguing that a relatively orderly existence can be obtained in communities and in organizations because they compel those who suffer from mindless hostility to express this indirectly in the form of a reasoned statement, which at once exposes and therefore removes the mindlessness from the situation, and permits everyone to seek a solution as if the hostility did not actually exist (although they know very well that it does). The front stage thus remains untainted and filled with people, who, when they are wearing community masks proclaim brotherly love and the impossibility of enmity, and who, when wearing organization hats, appear to take for granted the prevalence of rational behavior, unaffected by emotions and passions; in neither case need the actors countenance the existence of mindless hostility.

Under the Stage: Gossip

On the front stage parade people of kindly disposition (except, of course, towards those creatures which live beyond the boundaries of the community) and people who think before they act and who can reason out the consequences of different choices. These same people also hold resolutely to their principles, believing firmly (in our chosen cases) in the good university as a place of learning, *or* a collegiate institution, *or* an instrument to be used in the service of outsiders. Holding to these first principles is non-rational, because they cannot be justified; only asserted. Consequently, when people feel the need to make a deal which sacrifices some of these principles, they get off the front stage and go out of sight where they can behave in an 'unprincipled' fashion by making compromises. The front stage is the home of non-rationality and back stage is where reason takes over, and where adjustments are made to the inescapable demands of an outside world.

The principles asserted from the front stage are those of brotherly love and rational behavior. It is not done to use the front stage to proclaim enmity, except towards outsiders. But neither do personal animosities have any place on that backstage where compromise is made and bargains are struck: at least, if animosity gets there, it is a source of inefficiency.

Personal animosities have their own covert existence not

behind the scenes but, so to speak, under the stage. Thus we have three spheres of activity: up front people are proclaiming the principles by which they are 100 per cent guided; behind the scenes they reveal that in fact they are only 80 per cent guided by these principles, and someone perhaps is going to give them something in return for trading off the other 20 per cent; under the stage is the world where gossip and the dissemination of scandal take place. This third sphere (gossip and scandal-mongering) is the one in which mindless antagonisms are expressed: but the rules for their expression are such that the potentially harmful effect is to some extent controlled.

What features distinguish gossip both from public debate about principles and from unprincipled private dealing? When people retire behind the scenes and let it be know that, despite what they said in public, they are ready to make a deal, they are attempting to make a decision, to reach an agreed course of action. It is an instrumental occasion. Secondly, they are usually making the exchange with a rival, for whom, despite the implied trust of agreeing to a behind-the-scenes deal, they must still have some wariness. But when the same man goes into the corner to gossip with a crony, the exchange is not a matter of business and not—overtly at least—concerned in any direct way with reaching a decision. They are friends, amusing one another and perhaps making one another better informed about the people around them. Typically the talk is not restricted to any particular item of business, but ranges according to fancy, as if to make clear that gossip is a special form of a conversation, a diversion, an entertainment, a game.

But one would not need the word 'gossip' if it were no more than entertainment through conversation. Gossip, particularly when it takes the form of scandal, is intended to shape an attitude. It is like the speech-making and the sermonizing of the front stage, for these too are intended to shape attitudes. A discussion of the differences will bring out what is particularly significant in gossip.

In the affair of the experimental School of Education, which I described earlier, its Head made himself more than a few enemies, and he found himself under attack on such relatively public occasions as Senate meetings or in the deliberations of the Planning Council. Some articles, both hostile and in his defense appeared in the University newspaper. These events took place just before that strange interlude when it became the fashion at Senate meetings and other public gatherings to throw soft-boiled eggs into the fan, as P. G. Wodehouse puts it in his gentlemanly fashion, and the attacks, although harsh, were directed at performance and policy rather than at the person. They were allegations about inefficient systems of accounting; the policy which governed the allocation of bursaries was questioned; the methods of conducting examinations and consequently the results of those examinations were put into doubt. No one said that the Head was motivated by personal ambition, was using funds in a way that could be considered corrupt, and had wholly prostituted academic standards to serve his own advancement. At least they did not say so in public: they said it toward one another privately. His most bitter enemies, talking mostly to one another and discretely to those whom they thought might sympathize, also said things about his marital life, about his failings with his own children, and about his religion and his heritage. 'What else do you expect of (. . .)?' they said, and into that slot you can put whatever set of words will help preserve anonymity, like 'an Irish Catholic' or 'someone who never got a doctorate' or 'someone just out of analysis' or 'a queer like him'.

So there is one difference. Speaking in public you are expected to address yourself when talking of fellow members of the community or institution, to questions of principle and policy and performance. When you turn to gossip you can address the whole person: when you talk about what he has done, this is a prelude to and a support for a judgement on him as a man (or on her as a woman) and an invitation to the listener to agree that the same kind performance is likely in the future.

If you should ask why people did not stand up in public and say that the Head was corrupt, self interested, overly ambitious, academically meretricious, and an Irish Roman Catholic, only recently out of a padded cell, then the answer comes partly from commonsense and partly from a small section of anthropological writing, which by now has more or less achieved the status of commonsense.

Let us deal with the latter first. I am referring, of course, to the writings of Gluckman and Frankenberg and Elizabeth Colson, and some of my own:[10] if such things were said in public, then it would be impossible for those concerned ever to cooperate with one another, and since in communities such cooperation is a necessity, people hold back from calling a spade publicly a spade. This, of course, is an answer delivered from a distance through the spyglass of functionalism: whether or not those concerned have in mind the future of their community and continuing cooperation with those for whom they feel a mindless antagonism, remains doubtful. What is not doubtful is that if they do begin throwing eggs into the fan, then people around them will take steps to educate them into not doing so again.

There are also some other and more directly personal considerations which distinguish gossip from public utterances. By gossiping, that form of communication which is the hallmark of a community, the speaker avoids responsibility, evades accountability. Furthermore, the listener is expected to take the information on trust, not asking for evidence because it comes from a friend. We are reminded of the dean who accepts a friend's 'yes' or 'no' about a candidate, without asking for detailed evidence. The lack of accountability is further emphasized by the quality of 'mindlessness' or 'lack of purpose' which is lent by the myth that gossip is partly entertainment, rather than a serious activity with an effect on the real world.

In short, the gossiper sidesteps refutation, avoids the risk of direct public reprisal (like being taken to court for slander) and does not run the risk of losing public support by making public accusations which would rock the boat for everyone.[11] He even has the benefit of a trial run, for by gossiping and leaving to others the decision of whether or not they will hand it on, sometimes he is able to test the ground for a more open accusation. In the sphere of gossip, like the sphere where deals are made, one avoids publicity and accountability, not only because one is acting in defiance of public principles, but also because one is experimenting.

Having set up the picture of the man who deliberately gossips in order to see how strongly the wind is blowing in his favor (obviously a man who reasons and calculates is far removed from the person suffused with mindless antagonism with whom we began),[12] this is perhaps the place to remark that gossip also helps us let off steam. It can be an activity like swearing, or taking a cold shower when tempted by the devil in other forms, or kicking the dog or sticking pins into a wax doll. It all becomes wonderfully complicated, because the listener is left to decide whether the gossiper is relieving his feelings by venting them to a friend (a sign of trust), or whether he is using the friend as an instrument in a political campaign: it *is* complicated, because if the friend decides that the latter is the case, then the friendship has gone down one notch. It is like the picture of the painter painting a picture of a painter painting a picture of a painter and so on, and then trying to decide which of these images best represents reality.

Let us go back to the grosser level of functional analysis, and consider how far another suggestion of Max Gluckman applies in the context of universities. He said that, inasmuch as some rules on which community life depends are not codified and are sometimes not even articulated, they cannot be formally and openly sanctioned, either because they are too trivial for public attention or because they are so heinous that public consideration of them would be catastrophic.[13] So the housewife keeps her doorstep whitened and the brass knocker brightly polished, and her husband carefully modulates his relationship with the widow next door because both of them have in mind what the rest of the street would say if they did not. This is the sanction of 'people are beginning to talk . . .' No doubt such things occur in universities, but one is struck, in trying to find examples, by the opposite: the truly immense tolerance of eccentricity, so long as it is balanced by brilliance in research or teaching. A mind and intellect acknowledged to be truly fine can wipe clean almost any dirty slate and the Academy abounds in happy stories about the crazy colleague: like the man whose lectures in philosophy I once attended, a truly distinguished theologian, who expressed a strong difference of opinion with a visiting Bishop by going down on his knees and biting deeply into the Bishop's gaitered calf. Whether Irish Roman Catholic or Jew or Protestant, whether in or out of a padded cell, no one cared because his writings were said to be those of a genius.

To summarize so far. Gossip is the passing of information in such a way that the gossiper cannot be held responsible for what is said. He gossips not about policy and principles but about persons, and most of what he says is damaging since, other than in special circumstances, (as when one has something good to say about a public enemy) good things can be said in public. The gossiper may simply be letting off steam, like the philosopher who bit the Bishop's calf. He may be sending up a trial balloon to see whether or not he could make more open accusations. Gossip has the effect, in some situations, of pulling up short those who disregard accepted customs, of reminding them that they may be on the way to being considered a 'bad lot' and expelled from the community. Finally, gossip allows both the sanctioning and the experimentation without anyone having to take up a formal public position, without having to risk face, without putting other people into the position where they have no alternative but to fight or be defeated: in other words, all these warnings and experiments can go on without the danger of forcing people into public positions and so emphasizing differences in principle, which, from that point onwards, can be resolved only by a fight.

The Basic Lie and the Control of Information

I began by talking about mindless antagonisms, and how men were led into making arguments against a person, thus transforming him into an entity more immediate, more real, above all more readily attacked than the abstract sum of his performances and the policies which he supports. Both within communities and in organizations such hostility is deplored and much of this chapter has been taken up in describing ways in which the expression of this hostility is, so to speak, driven underground. The fully civilized man, the person who is not *sauvage,* has been educated into the white lie: into thinking twice before he tells the truth as he sees it, at least so far as it concerns other persons. If he does try to say such things in public, his opinion is likely to be written off as that of someone who is irresponsible if not crazy. He is forced to make his open complaint in such a way that the personal sting is taken out of it and the discussion can revert to the respectable level of performance and policy. If he does want to indulge himself in remarks about his enemy's ancestry or immoral behavior, he can only do so to a restricted audience, and, although it is commonly said that gossip spreads 'like wildfire', whether that is true or not, the information remains a kind of 'half-information', because it is unverified and because it is unsponsored.

Now, in conclusion, I will shift the emphasis and argue that although the myths that we have about gossip treats it as a feature deserving elimination, as a sign of a Fall from a more perfect world, nevertheless, no social world is even thinkable without the irresponsible circulation of information about persons. Up front is a daylight world based on the principle of brotherly love or on the principle of rational endeavor. But because principles may conflict, and because the conflict cannot be solved by reason, there is behind a twilight world where principles are compromised in the interest of getting something done, particularly when there are changes in the society's environment. I am now suggesting that there is a further sphere, which we can call night where information, mostly unflattering, is transmitted about persons. My argument will be that this sphere, too, has an adaptive function.

I will make the point by talking again about committees. The larger the committee, the more formal tends to be its deliberation. The debaters may score off one another, but this has to be done in the idiom of 'my honorable friend' and a personal attack must be delivered delicately and by innuendo. The reason for this is that the proper business of such committees is to consider policy and issue and principles, not persons.

As one moves to smaller committees, so the atmosphere changes, providing that—as is often the case—the committee is charged with working out the implementation of some agreed policy, and especially if it is engaged in selecting personnel to carry out the policy. These qualifications are in fact stages in moving from the world of abstract principle towards the world of doing, the infinitely complicated world of the administrator; complicated because it is a far from perfect meld of, or compromise between, different kinds of expertise. At this level committees are brought back to considering whole persons. The candidate may be well qualified by training and experience to run the committee on extra-mural education, but five years ago he ran away with the wife of a town councillor who happens to be the municipality's liaison man with the university. In recent years I have listened with wonder at the apparently interminable depths of the folk memory about personal failings, quarrels which took place many years ago but may still have a spark in them, personal quirks like loss of nerve, aggressiveness, tactlessness, obstinacy, and so on. Sometimes such information only comes out in a post-mortem into some spectacular failure. Such failures would be much more frequent if there were not this folklore of information about persons.

Of course, there are drawbacks. The stock of information is incomplete and often inaccurate, because there is no systematic way of keeping it up to date and checking its accuracy: and it is open to abuse, because a man can use it to put his enemies down when he is pretending to act in the general interest.[14] There is no solution to this: for if the information were codified and made publicly available, it would become impossible to look anyone else in the eye.

Conclusion

The point resembles that made earlier. The move from high principle and reasoned analysis in the direction of real life, where action has to be taken, is a move out of a rather clumsy world where people can pretend that the answers are known and easy, a crudely scientific world: at the lower level of action it is the whole rounded individual, the moral being complete with malice and misinformation and confusion, who must get things done. The happiest are those who can tolerate confusion: most of the time the tidy mind, if in touch with reality, must also be a discontented mind.

NOTES

1. See *Mair,* chapter 8. Her analysis of patronage in the royal courts of traditional African kingdoms can be taken up as a metaphor and applied to men who rule behind the scenes

in the world of business, science, the media and government. One of the many uncomplimentary books about Nixon is called *The Palace Guard.* For most English speakers a monarchy has some connotative simulacrum of respectability: an alternative metaphor is that of the criminal world, the boss and his henchmen.

2. See *Parsons* and *Platt.*
3. See note 9 of chapter 4.
4. See *Mayer,* p. 103.
5. The New Guinea 'big man' has become the epitome in anthropological writing of self-aggrandizement. The term has some of the connotations of 'hustler', discussed in note 6 of this chapter. An introduction to the subject of the big men in New Guinea can be obtained by consulting *Sahlins.*
6. 'Hustler' and 'popularizer' are both terms of denigration. They diverge and they come together in the following ways. The hustler is like a rate-buster: he offends community norms by exerting himself to achieve success more than do his colleagues and so he makes them feel uncomfortable. At one institution where I taught, it was the practice to put out each year an annual report, which included among other things a list of publications by faculty members during the preceding year. Most people, depending on their discipline, would show two or three papers in learned journals and perhaps every five to seven years, a book. But one member regularly filled two complete pages of the list, and appeared to be producing a book about once a year. He was a mild embarassment, and there was some light-hearted talk about vasectomy, but in fact he had to be treated as a curiosity rather than an object of hatred, because all that he wrote, while not exhibiting genius, was nevertheless academically very respectable: not a whiff of the popularizer about him.

But hustling in that style is uncommon. Generally the word suggests short cuts: someone so intent on success that he is unwilling to wait through the labors of slow recognition that is the best most scholars can expect, but instead becomes an assiduous man on committees, a dispenser of resources, an editor of books, and so, by degrees, he becomes also a popularizer. Such a man, it is generally felt, would be less polluting if he were to go straight into administration, and to dispense with the facade of a scholarly reputation for which he lacks the foundations.

7. 'Should' is used advisedly: sometimes the outcome is exactly the opposite. Those who could generally tolerate a relationship which was formal and indirect, may find that face-to-face contact points up hitherto concealed Satanic qualities in the other person. See the remarks on mindless enmity later in this chapter.

8. See *Coser,* p. 48.

9. When talking about these ideas I have met critics who point out with some fervor the fine things done in encounter groups and therapy groups, where the ethic is to let it all come out. Thus my defense of hypocrisy and reserve is not only old-fashioned, it is also a sign of being 'uptight' and very unhealthy. The answer is simple: therapy groups are for therapy, not for distributing scarce resources between claimants who all think they have a good case, nor for selecting a new dean of the graduate school, nor for deciding whether a colleague should be given tenure or terminated. Even the 'clearing the ground' argument seems to me spurious: total frankness may clear the ground, but it is also likely to leave the land sown with salt. The point is related to that made in note 7 of this chapter; consult also the works listed in note 10 of this chapter.

10. The references are *Colson,* 1953; *Frankenberg,* 1957; *Gluckman,* 1963; and *Bailey,* 1971 and 1973.

11. How does one protect oneself from gossip, or protect a friend? I think it is impossible, for the reasons given in this sentence. One can start a counter-campaign of slander and perhaps intimidate the other side, but that is a different matter: our question is how can one demonstrate that the content of gossip is untrue? Of course, much depends on what

is being said. The gossip may be that you no longer are seen in public with your wife because you are tom-catting elsewhere. You can nail the *fact* by being seen in public places with your wife. But the slippery part is in the *attribution of motives:* the 'real' reason may be that both of you have decided that restaurants charge too much and cocktail parties are a bore and home-cooking is better: this you can publicize only by saying it and there is no real defense against those who say that where there is smoke there is also a fire, and anyway, those who have tried her home-cooking would know better.

In Orissa in 1959 there were some political broadsheets and a few journals which carried articles about leading politicians of an unbelievably scurrilous quality. I asked one politician why he did not take them to court: he could have won a case simply by saying that there are not enough hours in the day or muscles in the body to indulge in all the curious habits that had been attributed to him. He said that, expense apart, such an action would give the libel more publicity and most people would believe that there was some truth in it: better to leave it in a poorly printed journal with a small circulation than project it into the headlines of the newspapers.

12. Such activities are much more sophisticated in fact than in my treatment of them. Gossip can be skilfully used, especially in private arenas but also sometimes before the public, without having to repeat the content. A hint or an allusion can be sufficient for the speaker to capitalize on everyone's knowledge of some colleague's frailties, and he need not describe those frailties. This is one of the several forms of double-talk which I have had to leave unexplored.

A second over-simplification has eliminated a range of variations in the content of gossip. The story of the man who bit the bishop's calf is gossip: but it is virtually without malice. Clearly the degree to which listeners judge that the story will hurt its subject will influence the gossiper's ability to get things out into the open. People often try to use this by prefacing some piece of egregious malice with the claim that they are about to communicate something hilarious.

13. See *Gluckman* 1972, p. xxiv.

14. See note 11 of this chapter.

CHAPTER SIX

Masks

Ten Masks

No effective politician presents his allies and his rivals with the rich indigestible confused complexity of his own true self: instead he uses a mask or affects a character.[1]

The metaphor of the drama suggested in the words 'mask' and 'character' should not be misunderstood. It is not that *all* the world is a stage, but only that *in the world of politics* no one ever wins without having at least some capacity to be a 'player'—to present in a bold, simple, indeed, caricatured fashion some side of himself or his policies that will captivate his supporters and intimidate his rivals. One should suppress the notion that this is 'mere hypocrisy' and therefore, if not unworthy of study, at least far short of 'true' study of 'real' politics. On the contrary, this is real politics: for when a man parades a mask he is attempting to take control by imposing on others his definition of the nature of men and the social world in which they live; that definition is condensed in the expression on the mask.

The first mask, appropriately so in the context of a university is that of REASON, who certainly displays 'the madness of the purely rational man' [2] because he believes that every problem has a solution, that this solution will be discovered through reasoned debate and reasoned argument, and, once discovered, will be accepted and implemented by everyone capable of reason, which means, in REASON's view, anyone who deserves to be his colleague in the university.

Someone, bandaging up the abrasions left by REASON's saw-toothed logic, remarked, 'There's a solution to every problem, according to REASON, even the parking problem'. Few people find it pleasant to thrash things out with him: a short sharp Socratic—but far from gentle—exchange demonstrates that one has not thought the matter through: then one is run over by a discourse which moves from first principles to recommended policy with the speed and force of an express train passing through a wayside station (Indeed, whether REASON or the express train, the effect is similar: conversation ceases.) REASON, however, seldom has his way. Once the train is through the station and vanishing to who-cares-where, normal businesslike interchange can start again. The causes of his ineffectiveness are several. Firstly, the solution offered by him, although following unswervingly and undisputably from his first assumptions, is frequently crazy. 'I think I follow your line or argument', people say, 'but it wouldn't work'. Other critics may directly question the primary assumption from which the reasoning began. (This is often very remote: a plan to install parking meters might start from an assumption about the aims of higher learning. Part of the pleasure in listening to REASON is the gazelle-like leap in his logic.) When REASON finds his assumptions questioned, he becomes impatient and may reassert his original assumption, or he may take another and contradictory assumption and lead his audience to just the same conclusion that he had reached before. Either way, he is impatient with argument about first principles and fundamental values (indeed he sometimes voices contempt for that kind of talk) and he devotes his energies to the chains of reasoning that lead from any old first principle to any old course of action.

REASON can be epitomized as a 'technician of the intellect'. Beauty for him lies in the intricacy of the machine and the moral question of what the machine does is of little interest. Secondly, and in another sense of the term 'moral', his outlook is amoral. He refuses to build into his calculation the full roundedness of human nature: jealousy, malice, love, personal ambition, and all the other irrational things, which in fact fuel the thinking machine, are disregarded. He refuses to see that decisions are the product not only of an orderly intellectual progress from premise to conclusion, but also of a compromise between conflicting interests. To put it less harshly, he is more concerned with his intellectual perception of order than with the application of that perception to the real world: thus he can stay short of political considerations. This, in the end, is why his advice is seldom put into practice: he does not stay around to fight for implementation, because he believes that his reasoned advice will sell itself to reasonable men, and if one is casting pearls one should not also be asked to blow them down the creature's throat.

The second mask is that of BUCK (the currency, not the animal) and in one important way he resembles REASON: he has an oversimplified view of human nature. He believes that anyone will do anything, if the price is right. REASON's opinion of his colleagues is the more flattering: they are Intellect writ large. For BUCK they are Stomach writ large.

BUCK, on one occasion, was taking part in a discussion of the following problem: universities give tenure to some of their faculty and this may tie up a position for as long as forty years; universities also desire to innovate and change and sometimes this entails a change of personnel. How is the contradiction resolved? BUCK had a case history from another university. The names of all those faculty members above or approaching the age of fifty-five, who were being paid less than the mean of their rank, were selected from the list by an administrator. This administrator concluded that these must be the inefficient and undesirable members of the faculty and he conducted what BUCK called an 'independent check' with the deans, who, wonderful to relate, produced virtually the same list of undesirable people. Someone present pointed out that this was hardly an independent check, since the deans in that institution had control over faculty advancement and promotion, but BUCK could not see the point and went on with—literally—shining eyes to explain the Machiavellian scheme put into practice by his administrator-hero. All these undesirables were offered the mean salary for that rank, providing they retired. The device BUCK explained, could be adjusted so as to cause one-fifth or one-third or the whole of a particular body of faculty to retire, apparently of their own volition, at whatever age was desired. It was, he said, 'just beautiful'.

There are some similarities between REASON and BUCK. Both care little which set of fundamental values appear to guide the enterprise—and both close their eyes to the many-sidedness of human beings. REASON has little interest in manipulating people, because they should all see reason anyway: on the other hand for BUCK manipulation is the name of the game (phrases like that and Nixon-type analogies from the sporting world abound in his talk) and the 'beauty' of the device which he outlined was nothing intrinsic but visible only in its puppet-like effects.

The third mask is that of SERMON. He sees himself as the guardian of our eternal verities. Neither he nor REASON hesitate to talk at one another, but neither do they listen, for where one begins the other leaves off. REASON is expert in unraveling the chains that bind first principle to plan of action: SERMON deals exclusively in first principle, and since, by definition, he has no anterior principles by which to justify them, his discourse contains little or no reasoning, and emerges from and is aimed at the heart rather than the head. 'It has long been our tradition that . . .'; 'The high standards which we have always maintained require . . .'; 'No decent person could contemplate . . .'; 'Others must share my great concern . . .' and so forth. SERMON considers that his colleague REASON is clever but not always good, because like a sophist he will defend the good and the bad with equal facility: he regards BUCK as both mindless and evil. In fact, none of them respects the others. BUCK considers his colleagues ineffective, mere spinners of words and helpless in the face of the real world. REASON categorizes BUCK as 'sub-university', a man who acts and implements, at best a facilitator for superior people who think. SERMON deals with things apparently of the mind, but in a way that is, in a quite literal sense, 'pre-logical': he deals with problems that are by definition insoluble (according to REASON), which is certainly an irrational way of spending one's time.

To summarize, REASON deals with the links which connect means and ends, but neither with the means nor the ends themselves; SERMON hammers away at the ends and BUCK manipulates men indirectly through impersonal devices and all three avoid being brought face-to-face with their fellow human beings.

Dealing with people-as-people is the strong point of the fourth mask STROKE. (His name refers to the action and not the affliction.) Like REASON, STROKE tends to shy away from discourse about first principles and eternal verities, and, when backed into a corner, will usually take refuge in one or another version of 'the greatest good of the greatest number', a sign that he wants to leave his options open to deal with the many-sided complexity of his particular colleagues. Like BUCK he is a manipulator of men (which makes a contrast between them and the other two) but he does not work through the remote control of indirect monetary incentives. He deals 'one-on-one', flattering, cajoling, threatening, altogether a craftsman-like performance shaped to suit the particular occasion and the particular customer. He lives in a personal world which he likes to keep warm, a world where people are made orderly by being 'stroked' into place. There is no single 'beautiful device' for making this happen, for the same simple reason that the drill which cuts into wood is blunted in stone and the drill which bores into stone gets clogged in wood; people, even fellow-academics, are as different as wood and stone.

Perhaps STROKE sounds so far the most amiable of the masks, but there are some black streaks in his character.

STROKE tends to suffer from a disease called 'near horizons'. His time is spent in small arenas, stroking and being treated in that way by others, and he runs the risk of becoming so much involved with the satisfactory arrangement of personal interaction that he may lose sight of the ends toward which this manipulation was first directed. He buys peace or achieves victory or evades humiliation in a small arena at the cost of creating chaos in some larger arena.[3] STROKE sometimes finds it hard to take hard decisions and, sooner than lose a friend, he may abandon a principle.

The 'short horizons' handicap comes out in another way that will be familiar to anthropologists. Because he deals so much with persons, and chooses to arrange his universe as a pattern of interpersonal deals, STROKE is prone to forget that certain events are the consequences of structural arrangements. If one believes that the world is to be set in order by stroking individuals, then when things go wrong that must be because the individual was wicked or filled with malice. STROKE, in fact, is a man who believes in witchcraft, although he is unlikely—unless an anthropologist—to understand that statement; indeed, he would feel himself insulted by it. Misfortunes are primarily the result of moral failings: if the persons concerned would only have the right attitude or take the trouble to understand, nothing would go wrong. If they choose to act otherwise, this could only be because they have a personal dislike for STROKE. Of course, he is often right—he has enemies—but (this STROKE finds hard to comprehend) there are role arrangements in any organization that must engender conflict even if the actors have been prestuffed with all the goodwill in the world.

One mask has indeed been 'prestuffed with all the goodwill in the world' and everyone is expected to love the wearer: he is SAINT. Like STROKE, but unlike REASON and BUCK and SERMON, he deals in the full rounded humanity of persons. Certainly he will put people before principles, and in his quiet way, he is totally unconcerned with organizational questions and efficient management. Indeed, without making a point of it, and without being demonstrative or militant or making any overt points at all, he can ravel up the once neat sleeve of bureaucratic procedures into a tangle that will take hours of other peoples' worry and hard work to bring back to order. There is a pleasing quality of innocence about SAINT: that the world might come to a stop if others did not clean up after him, is a thought that is never allowed into his mind, and he is given the small child's privilege of fouling the home, because he is so lovable and so innocent of any deliberate sabotage. The expression painted on his mask proclaims: 'Love me because I love you!'

One might think that such a man, patently unconcerned with deciding policy or wielding power, clearly without personal ambitions, ready to sacrifice his time to listen patiently and give comfort and counsel that is wise—or if stupid, at least untainted by some concealed self-interest—one might think that such a character must have a small part to play in the drama of politics. But such is not the case: he can, as I have said, twist into confusion the simplest procedures. (one of REASON's weaknesses is failure to make allowance in his plans for the factor of saintly confusion.) But there are also some positive things about SAINT. No organization can work without softening the rigidity of its rules and procedures in order to meet change and the unforeseen event, and the activities and example of SAINT are one among several ways of making this adaptive process more acceptable. Secondly, since no-one is allowed to hate the man wearing the mask of SAINT, he makes an ideal mediator, for he has no axes to grind and none to use on other people's plans and ambitions. Furthermore—perhaps an expression of the sense of utter helplessness that sometimes overcomes those who try by the use of reason alone to become masters of their fate—there is a myth that he, like Mrs. Moore in E.M. Forster's *Passage to India* or Mrs. Wilcox in *Howards End,* is in touch with a higher wisdom that is beyond reason; a useful reputation in any political arena.[4]

The sixth mask, although certainly unamiable, is, at least, when compared with SAINT, straightforward and uncomplicated in outlook, although the actions may be devious. He is BARON: the man with moustaches, with testicles, who in every situation sees but two possibilities: to screw or be screwed, and he aims to be the man who turns the screw. Like BUCK, he sees the world of politics revolving not around principles and policies, but around interests. Unlike BUCK, people for him are not to be indirectly manipulated by rewards so that they retain some simulacrum of self-respect but directly intimidated by the threat of punishment: the expression on the mask says: 'Do as I wish or suffer the consequences!' Like STROKE and SAINT but unlike BUCK, he lives in a highly personal world where the horizons are near, but, in contrast with SAINT, love and trust play no part, and life without a contest is no life at all—at least not for a real *man*. He too can be a bull in the china shop of bureaucratic orderliness, but, unlike SAINT, he is not indulged by his colleagues and his outlook on the world tends to be confirmed by his own experiences: as soon as he relaxes his hold on the screw, others will gladly turn it on him.

There is one mask which belongs in the same stable as REASON, but differs in that while REASON takes an artistic delight in sculpting his own chains of reasoning, this character buys what he needs in the supermarket of formulae: he is FORMULA. He believes not only that all problems have solutions, but also that these solutions already exist in the regulations and need only to be applied to particular situations. There is a curiously religious quality about this faith, reminiscent of SERMON, for once the formulae and procedures have been worked out they are seen as unalterable except by a great effort that is seldom, if ever, worth the trouble. At the lowest this is the petty bureaucrat who will not depart one inch from the rule: you cannot have money to buy your airplane ticket until you produce the receipt which shows you have bought it. Laboratories are built to house twenty-five students who must be supervised by a teaching assistant because they are handling dangerous apparatus: therefore the allocation in certain natural sciences must be one teaching assistant to every twenty-five students. The idea that a wall or two could be knocked down, or that supervision could still be adequate if the man in charge spent every alternate fifteen minutes in each room, is fiercely resisted just because it would alter an established practice. FORMULA along with SERMON are men who like to have their world secure, men who need the 'basic lie'. The final freedom is being able to bow gratefully to the demands of the system.

No one in touch with the world and people around him can be entirely a FORMULA. Even the most complete set of rules still leaves areas for choice and decisions have to be made. If you believe that such decisions are settled by discussion between reasonable men according to the principles of what is best for the whole institution, then you are like RATIONAL. He is a version of REASON, but superior in that he is willing to debate first principles and also is concerned about implementation and its effects. To every problem there is a best solution, although it might not be perfect. The principles taken into account may be those of the community, such as fair shares for all or Buggin's turn to get the medal; or they may also be principles characteristic of an organization, for example maintenance of the inward flow of resources, through teaching the maximum number of contented students or recruiting a brace or two more Nobel prize winners. RATIONAL believes in *numen,*[5] that the interests of the collectivity must prevail over sectarian interests and that, once people perceive what are the collectivity's interests, the decision will have been reached. This view combines the values of 'community' with the myth of a rational bureaucracy. It excludes any notion of continued competition and wholly ignores the possibility of irrational antagonism.

RATIONAL's myth stands in opposition to that of BARON.

BARON sees himself as a realist, serving the interest of a constituency rather than of the whole collectivity, in competition with other barons and likely to win so long as he displays sufficient *machismo* and sufficient cunning. He particularly enjoys grabbing nine-tenths of the pot for his own segment while making an argument that such an allocation is best for the collectivity as a whole. In BARON you will have recognized a caricature of the chairman of a department.

BARON, as I have just indicated, requires a normative facade. Whatever is in his heart, he loses the game if he advocates the interest of his own department without shame and without cover. Typically, he needs to use and perhaps be guided by certain well-known arguments about free enterprise. The greater part of all resources should be shared out between departments, and the departments should be given the responsibility for using them responsibly. If there is a debate about allocating money for teaching assistants, then some relatively simple formula like the number of undergraduates handled by that department should be used, and it should then be left to the departments to decide whether the assistants should be used in upper division or lower division courses, in discussion sections, or whatever else. The central authority should not attempt to place constraints on the resources it allocates, or should do so as little as possible, because there is such diversity between disciplines, even between courses, that any single procedure cannot be appropriate in all cases.

In brief, BARON's view is that a university essentially is a marketplace of interest groups, most of the time competing with one another for shares of a fixed pie (if one gets more the others get less) and that the themes of the rational bureaucracy are merely useful devices with which to discommode in argument one's opponents.

There is also a Runnymede version of the BARON myth. The argument that each little chiefdom is so different from the next that no centralized planning makes sense, and that each chief should be left to manage his own affairs is collectively voiced when the BARONS think that the central administration is grabbing too large a share of the spoils. Chairmen fiercely resist an argument that the centralized purchase and maintenance of projection equipment would be cheaper and more convenient than having each department do the job for itself because centralized control automatically leads to inefficiency, diminishes the sense of ownership and responsibility and increases the likelihood of waste.

Indeed, most departmental chairmen are suspicious of any move which cuts into departmental autonomy: evaluation of their curriculum, questioning their judgement on the appointment or advancement of faculty, and most of all taking resources away from them to place in a central pool under the control of the administration. Schemes to create a 'pool' of faculty posts, at the disposal of the administration to enable it to innovate, are looked on with dismay: so also are the 'interdisciplinary' teaching programs, especially those which somehow escape the control of any one department by being under the direction of a dean or some other administrative figure.

The analogy with Runnymede suggests that departmental chairmen get together in order to impose their will on the administration. In my experience this rarely happens, and the Runnymede feeling emerges in a generalized suspicion of the administration and in the view that it is just another, if larger, competitor in the arena. Certainly coalitions are formed between chairmen, some of them structured like the familiar division between the natural sciences, the social sciences, and the humanities. But a coalition of all together is likely to be a fragile thing if only because it is in fundamental contradiction with BARON's myth of how things really get done.

This brings us to another myth and another mask. STROKE believes that organizations (and communities) are in some ways like the human body. Taking plenty of exercise to the point of feeling the strain is said in middle age to produce a secondary set of channels for circulation and to diminish the chance of a heart attack. Organizations, STROKE believes, require the same kind of treatment: secondary informal channels of circulation must be developed in order to cope with blockages in the formal channels.

This is what Lucy Mair calls the politics of the royal court: a highly personal world in which favors are dispensed (or withheld) between patron and client, the typical interaction being either stroking or striking. The myth of the rational bureaucracy says that all allocations are done through rational open debate: this myth says that at least some part of the resources are kept out of the arena and held by the king. Their distribution is covert and the principles on which gifts are made (other than the maintenance of a patronage network) are very obscure.[6]

Let us call this the mask of PATRON. It says that resources are not distributed by rational principles, but through a network of cronies; nor are they distributed through open competition, but rather through an illicit influence-off-the-course system. The Runnymede picture of the king having more in his grasp than the barons find desirable is tacitly admitted by the PATRON myth.

As usual there is an antithesis. No organization can work without contingency funds and since these are held to meet unexpected situations or to seize unlooked-for opportunities, and such things have to be done quickly, their disposal has to be at the discretion of a PATRON: who, at most, should be called to account for what he has done only after the events.

This view can be advanced into a rather 'pure' form of community-thinking. When you select a leader, and you think that he is good and trustworthy, then he should be trusted. He has a kind of 'tenure', a long-term credit which preserves him from immediate day-to-day accounting and before you try to remove him he should in effect have committed the 'crime' of being a 'bad lot'. One of my colleagues formerly taught in a university which was a most authoritarian and very successful institution, where the president and the deans ruled and where his committee obligations might take up three hours a month. In fact the chiefs rarely asked for advice, and were not obliged to ask for it. Out of ten decisions, he said, he could live happily with about seven. Now he serves in a university where six or seven hours a week might be spent on one or another kind of advisory committee. Here too, out of every ten decisions, about seven he can live with. We are back to the view that one does not earn a higher degree and carry on research in astrophysics or Australian kinship systems in order to become a part-time administrator and an ineffective politician: leave it to those who want to do it, who (you believe) will do it well, and get on with your own work.

Finally, there is the mask of ROCK (and the name can suggest either boats or things thrown). ROCK is the champion of the oppressed: but he is by no means a defender of *lost* causes, since the oppressed whom he choses to represent are those classes in the nation and world who at the present time are rocking larger boats than universities. ROCK has extremist and activist tendencies: when thwarted, he makes loud accusations of oppression, colonialism, racism; he has been known to organize boycotts of other people's classes and on occasions he has attended classes given by those he regarded as traitors to the cause, and by heckling and organizing hand-clapping, disrupted them. He has left behind him a trail both of very angry persons and of academic hulks, those who suffered a loss of nerve. Some reviewers write glowing accounts of his fine teaching and of his research (although neither of these things is true), because it is in the short run cheaper to have a cynical disregard for standards and the welfare of the institution than to risk the consequences of ROCK ever finding out that you are not his friend.

The Features of Masks

A mask invites the audience to accept the wearer's definition of the nature of men and the social world in which they live. Each mask, with slogan-like simplicity, states how the world is and how it should be. These portraits display a variety of features, which can be used to point up differences and similarities between them. They contain statements about (1) human nature, and (2) about institutional arrangements, the degree of specificity varying from case to case.

Not surprisingly, there is no single persuasive set of features which will do the job. The difficulty is not simply that well-known 'God's truth' and 'hocus-pocus'.[7] It is compounded by the fact that we are dealing with political interactions, and so with assertions which themselves start from irreconciliable contradictions between fundamental principles. Thus we can make no claim (although the actors do) that one particular analysis presents what people 'really' think: that *this* analysis alone has 'psychological reality'. It may have for the wearer of a particular mask (or may not, since the political arena allows bluff and hypocrisy): it certainly does not for all the wearers of masks. Later I will argue against any attempt to get at 'real' persons and 'real' motives. Given that argument one cannot use the criterion of 'psychological reality' to pick out the *one* best set of features.

The analysis presented in Chart 1 seems to me to be that which is most likely to provide a useful guide, given our interests. For example, the contradiction between community values and organizational values (1 and 2 on the chart) has turned out to be a dominant theme (dominant in the sense that the distinction is not only considered as important by the actors, but also arises over a wide variety of situations). For that reason I present it as the apical discrimination. This particular scheme of classification will then be augmented by discussing certain features which are present in the scheme but are not given prominence.

CHART 1

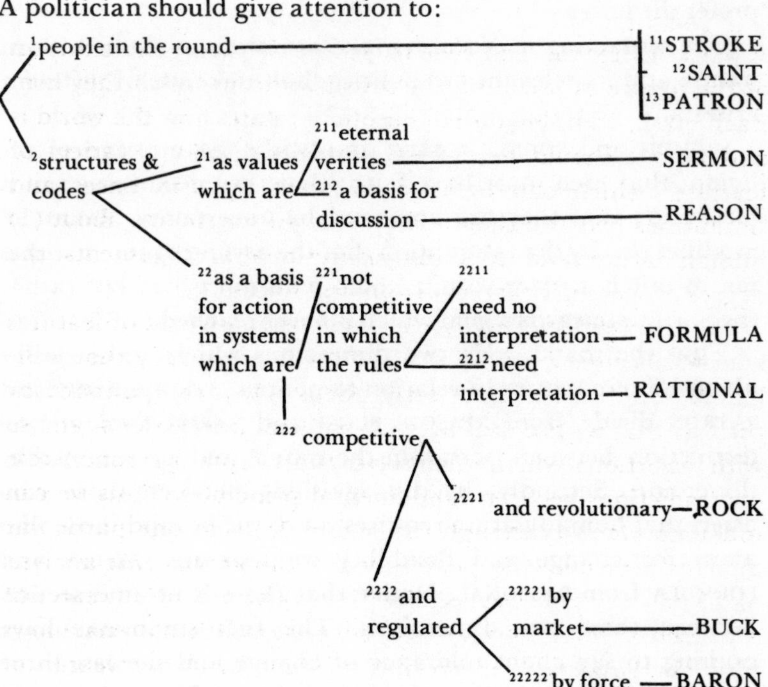

The main division in the diagram is between those masks which imply that in the context of politics the most important feature of human nature is the wish to be treated as a moral being, as an end in oneself, a complex person rather than as an instrument serving some institutional design. STROKE, SAINT and PATRON all carry this message and by implication assert that other masks (those listed under heading 2) are to be condemned, because the wearers 'have no heart.'

By contrast the three masks REASON, BUCK, and BARON imply that in the context of politics human nature is a simple one-dimensional affair. For REASON all one needs to know is that men can think; for BARON, that they can be moved by fear; and for BUCK, that they can balance out costs and benefits and prefer the latter.

The remaining masks also make assumptions about human nature and its relevance to politics, but make use of different criteria.

SERMON and FORMULA carry implicitly the message of religion: that men must have faith; that they need to accept a 'basic lie'; that they are unnerved by uncertainty. RATIONAL modifies this by the assumption that the asylum of the sacred is not so much a place within which man must live, but rather the journey towards a goal which is never reached.

Thus the masks code two dimensions which make claims about human nature in relation to politics. STROKE, SAINT and PATRON divide from REASON, BUCK, and BARON through the distinction between person-in-the-round and person-in-one-dimension. Secondly, by distinguishing between those who assert that human nature requires the 'basic lie' and those who allow for change and flexibility we separate SERMON and FORMULA from RATIONAL. Notice that there is no intersection between these two dimensions. The first six masks have nothing to say about tolerance of change and the last three have nothing to say about the roundedness of human nature. If one recalls that the salient characteristic of all masks is their simplicity, and secondly, that any field of political interaction contains contradictions, one should not be surprised at an absence of intersection: some people arguing about whether apples are red or green and other people arguing about how long they can be kept in store. Notice that in each case there can be communication—at least sensible communication—only within the same set. Potentially, of course, there could be an intersection, but about it the masks, being simple things, have nothing to say.

I will argue later that STROKE particularly (and I have already argued the same of SAINT) is likely to be effective in bringing about change. But the features of the masks themselves do not allow us to see this: it becomes apparent only when we have examined other features which distinguish arenas or stages, a question to be taken up elsewhere.

It is not surprising, also, that those masks which imply a relatively simple definition of human nature (fixated upon change or the lack of it, profit, fear, or thinking) are also those which have statements to make about institutional structures, codes and processes. It is true that STROKE, SAINT and PATRON imply the importance of community rather than organization (see chapter two) but this message is not painted clearly on the mask, which in each case deals explicitly with interpersonal relations rather than institutional forms. (Once again the arena dimension will be needed to make the connection.)

The four masks, SERMON, REASON, FORMULA and RATIONAL are relatively unspecific about institutional arrangements when compared to the remaining three, ROCK, BUCK and BARON (and, indeed, PATRON also about whom more in a moment). One can sermonize or reason about, expound or seek to adjust the regulations of any kind of institution. All these four masks imply that an institutional arrangement exists: the latter pair, FORMULA and RATIONAL further define the institution as being not primarily moved by competition: but beyond that point they are unspecific. They leave open stipulations which are made by the other masks: by BARON (and PATRON) that an important institutional feature is hierarchy; by BUCK that institutional arrangements are rendered orderly by impersonal forces; by BARON that, on the contrary, men are in charge of their own destinies; and by ROCK that whatever the institutional arrangements are now, they should be different.

To summarize, the masks vary in the degree to which they stipulate institutional arrangements. The three masks coded under figure 1 say nothing directly about institutions, except in the case of PATRON which stipulates hierarchy. Those masks which are coded under figure 2 fall into three categories. SERMON and REASON stipulate nothing institutional, except that there is an institutional arrangement about which to sermonize or on the basis of which to exercise reason. In the second category FORMULA and RATIONAL stipulate that such institutional arrangements should be regarded as a basis for action and considered to work without competition. In the third category competition is assumed, ROCK taking for granted that action will take the form of opposing the existing system; BUCK seeing the system regulated by impersonal forces in contrast to BARON who sees what order there is as the product of men striving to fulfill—and therefore in control of—their own destiny.

I have described certain features which are left obscured by the chart. These, together with the features which were used to give shape to the chart, will be considered again after other variables which concern who may wear what mask and in what situations, have been taken into account.

Masks and Persons

The metaphor of the mask exemplified by REASON, SERMON, BARON, BUCK, SAINT, STROKE, FORMULA, RATIONAL, PATRON, and ROCK may suggest that as the mask is superficial, so also must be the analysis. The mask belongs on the stage or at the time of Carnival, when people try to push out of sight the 'real' world in which they live, and so, by talking of masks, we move into a world of triviality, of make-believe, where men may find emotional release but from which, if they are to survive, they must return to face a 'real' world. What is truth and what is reality are questions not to be asked in jest, but this is not the occasion to stay for an answer; the problem belongs to the whole enquiry rather than to this particular part of it, and is taken up elsewhere.

In some ways the metaphor is appropriate. Masks are made large, their colors bold, their features simplified so that even standing at a distance the play-goer can see what Thespis intended this character to be. So it is with politics: when on the front stage, subtlety, ambivalence, qualifications, and the delicate touch are out of place because the audience cannot see them and if it could, would only be confused.

Secondly the metaphor of the mask appeals because it leads away from an enquiry into what 'really' motivates politicians. This question will not be asked. Our interest is in the range of masks available, in identifying the context into which particular masks fit, in finding rules for changing masks and for combining one with another, and in identifying the qualifications one needs to wear a particular mask without exciting disbelief or derision from the audience. What psychological factors dispose a particular *individual* to pick up one type of mask rather than another, is a question for others. When the choice is inappropriate (as with those who rush happily to martyrdom in defense of causes already lost), there are consequences, and these consequences are part of our analysis. But whether the martyr is a martyr because of infantile experiences with father, mother, nurse, or because of the way his glands work is not our question. *For this enquiry,* when all the masks have been stripped away, nothing is left.

That statement can cause confusion. Unfortunately, the word 'mask' connotes, indeed demands, someone to wear it, someone behind it, and our disposition and culture lead us to think of this someone as more complex, more interesting, and above all more valuable than the cheap and crudely painted artifact of linen or paper.[8] We want to find that there is an actor wearing the mask, and, much as we may be thrilled by his performance, at least for some people an even greater thrill is to meet him ' in the flesh'; that is, without his mask. To me it seems a strange illusion to expect an actor—or indeed anyone else—to be seen without a mask: what the fans see at the stage door is, of course, another mask. When in Bombay the lady in the black gown that covers her from head to foot, the *burka,* lifts the hem to step into the carriage and you catch sight of a trim nylon-clad ankle and a court shoe, do not think that you have seen the 'real' lady: only another of her masks.

At this point the metaphor, because it suggests an actor (a

flesh and blood reality which exists apart from its presentations), fails: but the line of argument can be maintained. The convenience of the English language will frequently require the noun 'actor,' but in effect the actor is a relationship between one mask and another mask or a set of masks. So far as the analysis of a political culture is concerned, a statement about an actor wearing the wrong mask or adroitly changing masks or having such a poor wardrobe of masks that he cannot adapt to a changing situation—all these statements in fact are about relationships between either one kind of mask and another or between masks and varying situations. For example, any actor who tries to play REASON and BARON on the same occasion, or too quickly in succession, will confuse his audience and not succeed in manipulating them: in the same way BARON is a poor mask to wear in a situation which calls for mediation, although it may be good for settling disputes in other ways: banging heads together. The individual wearing these masks is not an essential part of these statements, at least in this kind of analysis; merely the most convenient way of indicating relationships available in the English language.

There is one more complication. The word 'mask' in the context of the drama or of Carnival, suggests that the masks are 'properties' (in the stage sense of the word) and lie around in cupboards or hung on racks until they are needed, inanimate things, easily assumed, easily discarded. But in the context of politics, the word must have a rather different meaning: masks sometimes get to be like plastic teeth, or a toupee or dyed hair or a wig, a fixture which , if removed, and replaced by something else (gold teeth, a bald spot or a wig of different hue) will cause consternation in the audience. The costs and benefits in politics of becoming 'typed' (again in the stage sense) as against an infinite versatility will be reckoned in the next chapter, in discussing the significance of doing the unexpected.

NOTES

1. I have found among some of those who listened to these ideas a curious aversion from the word 'mask', an insistence that such hypocritical behavior was most undesirable, probably unimportant because rarely practised, and certainly not something to be talked about openly in respectable company. The significance of this sentiment is discussed elsewhere. At this point my purpose is to help the reader not to react to the description of masks which follows in the manner of an otherwise intelligent colleague, who said, 'People are more complicated than that'.

Certainly there is a problem in relating 'mask' to 'person'. Note 8 of this chapter faces it: here it is enough to quote a discussion of Ben Jonson and his 'humours', a word which comes close to my 'mask': ' . . . a humour character . . . is . . . allegorical, a vehicle for moral judgement, not a rounded portrait; not so much a man possessed by a quality as the quality itself embodied in the man.' (*Salingar,* pp. 79–80).

This act of abstraction, from the rounded person to the abstract quality, must be made not only by the writer seeking to make a moral comment, but also by anyone who wishes to make his view prevail, that is, by any politician.

2. This arresting phrase is taken from *Pritchett,* p. 23.

3. See the interesting discussion of the politics of wartime science in Britain in *Frankenberg,* 1972. The point about hard decisions is made on p. 277.

4. The cloud of other worldliness—and hence unworldliness—which our culture and other cultures too (see, for example, the descriptions of a Saint in *Barth*) hangs around its saintly public figures makes us think that saintly charisma and a talent for organization must be in complementary distribution: the presence of one is a clear indication of the absence of the other talent. The administrative chaos which followed in the wake of Vinoba Bhave's *gramdan* campaigns in Orissa in the 1950's seems proof of this. Nevertheless the

complementary distribution is more a fact of culture than a statement about personality. Gandhi, the greatest of them all, was no unworldly simpleton when it came to political manoeuvre; and, on another level, the rash of money-making divines which spots the face of American religion indicates more than a little administrative talent. The trick, of course, is to segregate the activites and have someone else than the charismatic leader be seen to do the administrative work.

Every leader should appear to have a line open to goodness, truth and beauty: but, except perhaps in the case of a few college presidents of bygone generations, most academic leaders have a very small fingerhold on those eternal verities and, if they are respected, it is likely to be for a combination of being smart, ruthless and effective: the charisma, if that is the word, of Attila the Hun, Shaka Zulu or Charles de Gaulle rather than of Gandhi.

Those who have only their devotion to the eternal verities and no capacity to get things done, will not be leaders in the academic world, although they may get their way over particular issues. In other words, the academic politician should use this mask only with the greatest discretion.

5. See note 9 in chapter 4.

6. See note 1 in chapter 5.

7. The reference is to *Burling*. See also the rejoinders, under *Hymes* and *Frake*.

8. The classic statement in anthropology, distinguishing two senses of 'character' is to be found in *Mauss*. On p. 277 he discusses the Latin *persona* and the Greek πρόσωπον thus 'À côté, le mot de *persona*, personnage artificiel, masque et rôle de comédie et de tragédie, de la fourberie, de l'hypocrisie—d'étranger au "moi"—continuait son chemin. Mais le caractère personnel du droit était fondé, et *persona* était aussi devenu synonyme de la vraie nature de l'individu.' and for πρόσωπον : 'Le mot πρόσωπον avait bien le même sens que *persona*, masque; mais violà qu'il peut aussi signifier le personnage que chacun est et veut être, son caractère (les

deux mots sont liés souvent), la veritable face. On étend le mot πρόσωπον à l'individu dans sa nature nue, tout masque arraché, et, en face, on garde le sens l'artifice: le sens de ce qui est l'intimité de cette personne et le sens de ce qui est personnage'.

Mauss is interested in the way in which cultures have, so to speak, evolved beyond the phenomenal, a man's appearances, (what I am calling here— like Mauss—his masks) towards the notion of some abstract unity behind the appearances and towards its reification as a social person or an individual. I have selected two quotations which emphasize the continued use, side by side, of two essentially opposed meanings contained within a single term—*personnage, caractère,* character, *persona,* and πρόσωπον : character as in a play opposed to character as some inner core of personality. 'Mask', unlike its Latin and Greek equivalents *persona* and πρόσωπον , is unambiguously applied to the surface and never to the supposed inner psychological reality.

My interest is in the political significance of this distinction, especially in the ambiguity of some of the terms. At various points in the text the following propositions are made:

(a) The search for the 'real person' behind the appearances is a part of that 'basic lie' through which people make stable sense of an unstable world. Hence the disdain for 'mask'. Hence also the kudos for those who can present themselves *tout masque arraché,* like Bert in chapter 7.

(b) The 'real person' *tout masque arraché, la veritable face* is, I maintain, itself a mask. It is part of a public myth about the nature of the good community, where everyone has confidence in everyone else and everyone, so to speak, has tenure, and no one ever need have secrets from anyone else. Communities, the myth maintains, are intolerant of masked performances because people deal with one another as moral beings and do not use one another as instruments. Expressions of admiration which one sometimes hears for 'a skilled performance' in a council or a meeting are certainly made by someone wearing an organization hat.

One can reach the same conclusion by a slightly different route. To wear a mask is to attempt to manipulate another person by getting him to adopt the definition of the situation presented in the mask. The victim is being used to achieve some extrinsic end; but the relationship which is the archetype of a community carries an intrinsic regard. One should not forget that these are competitive situations and that Jack's claim to have an intrinsic and wholly moral tie with Jill, may be countered by Jill's assumption that this is just his way of getting out of paying his share in what is essentially a contractual relationship. So the claim to be without a mask may be rejected as a form of 'moral blackmail'.

CHAPTER SEVEN

The Unexpected

Three Anecdotes

I begin with a miscellany of ethnography, not all of it connected, other than in an allegorical way, with life in universities.

In a farmyard in the Australian outback the old rooster, still the stronger in beak and claw, stands triumphantly on the dung hill, having reasserted his dominance over the young rooster. 'But at least I can run faster', says the young rooster. So they fall to arguing, and eventually decide to race around the farmyard, the young rooster to receive a start of two yards. Off they go, and round and round, the young rooster squawking loudly and the old one slowly gaining upon him, when suddenly—Bang!—the farmer lowers his shotgun, picks up the carcase of the old rooster, and takes it into the kitchen. The younger rooster climbs on the dung hill, and though weary of leg, begins contentedly to eye the hens. In the kitchen the farmer talks to his wife, 'Who would have thought it? After all these years, and he turns out to be a lousy poofter!'

From this you may conclude that in Australia as elsewhere roosters which have homosexual tendencies are not in favor. You might also reflect on the political sagacity to be found in young roosters. What the situation has to do with universities, we will come to later.

The second piece of ethnography is about one of those heroes of our time, a vice-chancellor in the age of student unrest. The particular occasion for discontent was unusually straightforward, concrete and rational. Postgraduate students preferred to live on campus in university apartments rather than in the somewhat distant town, but found it more and more difficult as inflation caused the rents to rise. They assembled to protest and the vice-chancellor agreed to discuss the matter with them. He was small, slightly-built, thin-lipped, always neatly but unostentatiously dressed, with a precise mind, a slightly acid sense of humor, a man experienced and skilled in argument, utterly without flamboyancy and wholly lacking in the common touch: respected but not loved.

For almost an hour the discussion went on, becoming increasingly constructive as each side acknowledged comprehension of the other's constraints, and perhaps getting within sight of a solution acceptable to all, when suddenly one student stood up and said loudly and clearly, 'F*** you, Cripps!' (That is a *nom de guerre* for the vice-chancellor.)

The move was quite unexpected, and perpetrated probably by someone who found conflict intrinsically interesting and who was therefore reluctant to see it ended. Most of the audience was surprised, and they sat there silenced for the moment.

The vice-chancellor, however, was not at a loss for words. His face turned puce and he seemed to swell to twice his normal size; he seized the microphone from the table in front of him and snarled into it, 'And the horse you came in on!', which is not an easy phrase to snarl. But he did: and then he walked out.

The students might just have seen the Thames run backwards up to Windsor: they understood neither the phrase nor the situation and they dispersed like rioters in a thunderstorm.

The third piece of ethnography is a small remembrance of what happened one hot summer's day in the headmaster's study, where the five members of the upper division of the classical sixth form had assembled to continue their discussion of the *Apologia*. Just before the lesson began, while the headmaster was still sorting out his books and notes, one of the class rose from the table, walked across the room, opened a window, and returned to his seat. After a moment the headmaster looked up and said, 'Jones, you have my permission to *have* opened the window.'

Jones smiled, uneasily, uncertain whether he should acknowledge a rebuke or just another of those feeble jokes to which teachers of the classics become addicted. It was both a rebuke and a joke, but Jones did not know how to respond appropriately; a riposte which capped the headmaster's verbal play, *might*, if it was clever enough and since this was, after all, the sixth form, have earned the headmaster's approval; on the other hand, it might have been construed as insolence. The headmaster was practicing, in effect, a gentle and refined form of bullying.

In what follows some of the dimensions which run across these three pieces of ethnography will be considered.

Here now is a story to provide flesh for the bones of analysis. It concerns first the situations which determine what masks are appropriate and, secondly, the complementary and contradictory relationships between different kinds of mask.

A Versatile Man

The individual (or, to be consistent, the collection of masks) who is the hero of this story must be called Joe or Fred or Bert and not, for reasons that will become clear in a moment, Claude or Peregrine or Hubert or Julian. Let us call him Bert. He was born not long after the First World War into a working-class family in the north of England. Like his father he became a coal miner and his formal education ceased at the age of fourteen when he left school to start work at the mine and eventually go down the pit. When the Second World War came he continued to work down the pit—a reserved occupation—until Dunkirk, when he managed to enlist in the army, becoming a signaller. He served for a short time in India, where he saw no action, and then fought in the campaigns in North Africa and in Italy, surviving, rising through the ranks, and eventually receiving a commission. He was demobilized in 1946 with the rank of Captain.

It would be unfair to call Bert a drop-out from the educational system, for at the age of fourteen there was no way in which he could have continued. There were scholarships, but not so many, and in any case, Bert developed intellectual interests too late in life to take advantage of the State Scholarship system. But during his last year in the army, having much time to himself and encouraged by others, he was able to obtain the various academic certificates which made it possible, with the help of the grants available to ex-servicemen, to go to a university and take a degree. He became an economist, took a higher degree and eventually found himself teaching in a university.

By the time we meet him Bert was firmly in control of his world. His field was development economics and he had become expert on a particular region of what, at that time, was about to be called the Third World. His publications had earned him a solid, although not spectacular, reputation. He was unfashionably—and paradoxically given his background—inclined towards private enterprise, to the criterion of profit, individual initiative and away from socialism and state-run enterprises. On the whole, he believed, people should be given a chance to make their own way in the world. He was ready to argue this point with force, whenever he felt that the effort would be worthwhile.

His reputation as a man of initiative and an efficient builder and administrator was very high indeed. He was called upon frequently to be a consultant both to Ministries of Government and to international agencies. He had served on various nationwide educational committees, on which he had the reputation of being a forceful and effective man, who would stand no nonsense, even overbearing and sometimes unduly aggressive, particularly when meeting people for the first time or when new resources and opportunities were being made available. At all times he was ready, when it seemed of advantage to do so, to give people the rough edge of his tongue: in short, he was most often found wearing the mask of BARON.

But he could wear other masks too. As an economist and a true believer in the profit motive, he could be found behaving like BUCK, arguing both on public occasions and in small committees that individual enterprise should be freely encouraged by the appropriate rewards and penalities. He could preach a sermon in public or stroke people towards his point of view in private. Finally there was the not unexpected folklore of the kind heart that lay behind the rough exterior, and stories of his occasional acts of kindness, particularly in defense of the persecuted, enabled him on rare occasions to assume the mask of SAINT. In fact, the only mask which was not in his wardrobe was that of REASON.

The occasion which is the point of this story was apparently one of his rare lapses, when he failed to match mask with situation. Normally he did this with uncanny accuracy and completeness, even his speech changing to match the mask. He had never eliminated north-country vowels, but these and the vocabulary of the common people were least noticeable when he played BUCK or SERMON. Confronting a rival in public or private in the guise of BARON his north-country origin became more pronounced, both in the way he spoke and the phrases which he used. Acting in small groups, or one-on-one, he spoke as one spoke to friends back in the place from where he came and those tortured vowels and the stiff limited vocabulary, which he affected when first commissioned, were not to be heard.

The occasion was a meeting of a planning committee. The subject under discussion was a suggestion from the Ministry of Education that universities should reserve a percentage of their places for late developers, for men and women who had terminated their formal education early, had none of the certificates required for university admission, but appeared to have both the ability and the requisite motivation. The suggestion was accompanied, in BUCK fashion, by a promise that the Ministry would see that those universities which followed it would be substantially rewarded: by implication, those which did not might be penalized.

The suggestion received a somewhat negative reception. There was some talk about lowering of scholarly standards by the admission of 'sub-university material': others, less hard-nosed, anticipated difficulties for older students, perhaps with family responsibilities, long out of the harshly competitive surroundings of the sixth forms from which the younger students had recently emerged. But this was a planning committee, a set of people who defined themselves as realists, unwilling to spend much time talking about principles or standards, or the psychological and personal difficulties which older students might encounter. The discussion soon centered in upon what was for them the one real issue in the business: What was in it for the university if it adopted the scheme, and what would it lose if it did not? Whatever intrinsic merits or demerits the scheme might have were not debated; only its pay-off. So they went on for about ten minutes, Bert, despite his expertise in economic questions, taking no part in the discussion.

Then, suddenly, Bert intervened. He used his SERMON voice and SERMON vocabulary: 'I am distressed to hear the discussion take this form. Opportunities in this country are not open to all, are not decided on merit alone, and here we are offered a chance to provide some small remedy. The proposal is intrinsically a good one and we should accept it. It saddens me to find us talking about the entirely secondary issue of whether or not we would make a profit out of the scheme'.

There was a silence, which soon developed into an embarrassed silence, and then someone broke it by saying, 'I have to agree with that'; there were other murmurs of agreement and the committee decided to recommend the adoption of the Ministry scheme.

Why did no one turn on a debate? Bert had his enemies, on that committee as elsewhere, including some who, almost by reflex, set themselves in opposition to whatever Bert supported. No one can spend most of his time being BARON without creating a coterie of adversaries, and among them were a few relics of a past age believing that there was no place in a university for someone who habitually shortened his vowels and dropped his aitches. But no one said a word.

There might have been a debate, not to say an argument, if Bert had chosen to wear his normal mask of BARON. In that case he would not have said that he was 'distressed' but he would have used the word 'disgusted' or something stronger. He would have challenged those who were reluctant to accept the Ministry's suggestion and threatened them and perhaps deliberately attempted to provoke a riposte in the form of *argumentum ad hominem*: 'That would only be a way of getting more people like you into the university!' Bert would certainly have profited from such incautious abuse, because such statements can be made in the gossip channels but cause those who speak that way in public to lose respect.

But Bert's origins were certainly part of an unspoken communication. That, indeed, was one cause for the embarrassed silence. Bert was a member of the community, tenured in all senses of that word, and there was an uneasy feeling that to enlarge upon the earlier murmurs about such people being 'sub-university' could turn out to be too direct an attack upon Bert himself. There were others besides Bert with such origins, but most of them more chipped to a shape that would fit the mold of the middle class. By that time—and in that university at least—it was not done to speak openly and disparagingly about the class origins of one's colleagues.

The third reason for the embarrassment, which allowed the recommendation to slip through without further debate, was the appearance of a SERMON mask in a committee which prided itself on being realistic and on getting things done rather than on debate. People who were habitual sermonizers were not invited to join that committee, and the occasional lapse into sermonizing would be met with a few testy comments ('Yes, yes, quite! I am sure we are all agreed about that!') and an appeal to get back to business. On other occasions, if an old hand launched himself into a sermon, the others would look at one another with an expression equivalent to the forefinger held on the side of one's nose (never, of course, indulging in anything so blatant and vulgar) as if to say 'Watch him! He's up to some trick!' But on this occasion Bert, whether he knew what he was doing or not, had their legs off before they could move because his intervention was so totally 'out of character'. On that occasion he won: but such tactics are for use only on very rare occasions, because Bert had achieved something equivalent to the four-minute-mile in committee behavior: he had successfully worn the mask which claims, 'Look! You are seeing me without a mask!' Of course they were not; but one of the strongest norms of community living is that the man who is believed to have put aside all his masks and exposed the naked breast of his true self is on no account to be attacked.[1] For obvious reasons, if he does this once a week, the audience can no longer believe that this is not a mask. Sincerity is the *occasional* performance of the unexpected.

Out of this story emerge the following topics. Firstly there is some kind of fit between particular masks and particular arenas: for example, the planning committee is not habituated to enjoying the rhetoric of SERMON. Secondly, while a person can change masks, those which he habitually wears will arouse expectations in the audience and make it harder for him to wear new masks without exciting apprehension or ridicule. Thirdly, in addition to the constraints of situation, different actors have access to different wardrobes: Bert commanded an unusually wide range of masks, but some of his colleagues had only one. Combinations of masks will be discussed later: we now consider the relationship between mask and situation.

Mask and Context

The analysis requires the distinction between occasions for conducting politics which are public and those which are relatively private. The former arena is the place where principles and policies are announced, where the issues are simplified down to the point of caricature and slogan, and where a discourse about persons (except when they are used to symbolize a principle) is not usually acceptable. By contrast the private arena is unprincipled: a place for enlisting the support of individuals by striking individual bargains (by trading off a little of one ideology against another or in more material ways); a place for mediation, where rivals try to escape the heavy costs of outright conflict by reaching compromise; and thirdly, a place where the contestants keep their principles out of sight, and perhaps out of mind, and deal with the full roundedness of the person whether friend or enemy.

Despite the example of Bert's versatility, and despite the success of his flagrant violation of the grammatical rules of mask and context (sermonizing in front of cynics and realists), it is clear that some masks are well suited to one arena and ill-adapted to the other. In some cases the connection is obvious: sermonizing is not usually effective in private committees, because SERMON preaches about issues which private committees tend to take for granted, and he uses up time which might be better spent in getting things done. For the same reason in such committees there is a low tolerance for REASON because his discourses seemed to have nothing to contribute to problems of implementation. The controlling division is between making and implementing policy.

Since private committees can better consider persons and interactions between persons (which have to take place if policies are to be implemented), the masks which are effective are those of STROKE, BARON, SAINT, PATRON, and BUCK. This does not mean that such committees are entirely concerned with 'what will fly' rather than 'what is right' or 'what the regulations prescribe': only that after these external normative constraints have been taken into account, there has to be a discussion about who will do the job and how it should be done. Both in influencing fellow members of the committee, and in forecasting how people will act when asked to carry out whatever policy is laid down, those masks are likely to be assumed.

Thus, BARON may browbeat those who differ: 'I think that course would be very unwise, and I would certainly be obliged to oppose it with all the force at my disposal'. Or he may, more generally, try to persuade his fellow committee members that they live in a world of 'turn the screw or have it turned on you'. He might, for example, say: 'Above all we have to decide firmly on what should be done, and insist that it is carried out. The only thing that this place really understands is strength, and once people begin to think that you are weak or ineffective, you can expect no mercy from them'. BUCK, too, can operate in private arenas in just the same way as BARON: the latter believes that people respond to intimidation, and the former that they respond to rewards, or the threat of losses.

SAINT also has a role in the private arena. Certainly those who adopt one of the other masks are unlikely to accept his definition of other people: that they are essentially good people, respecting one another above all else and ready to sacrifice interests or principles in order to assist a colleague. But SAINT is the mask which gives the right to propose a compromise either between members of the committee who are in disagreement with one another, or between the committee as a whole and some outside rival; unlike BARON he has no face to lose by doing so, and, unlike BUCK (but like STROKE), he has no principles to be watered down by admitting that men are moved by something in addition to profit. (Also, as mentioned, he touches the hems of the robe worn by God, a possible source of divine optimism which, particularly when things go badly, even BUCK and BARON need.)

The masks of REASON and SERMON can be worn effectively (other than on very rare occasions) only in public arenas, because such men deal in principles and are far from the constraints of implementation. There is no place in such arenas for the mask of STROKE, for he deals one-to-one, and the vocabulary of flattery, which in private can be tailored to suit each individual, in public becomes embarrassing and is likely to arouse envy or derision, which the recipient can escape only with that convenient American word, 'Shucks!' The other three characters, however, all have something which they can parade in public arenas. BARON comes into his own when the public arena ceases to be an arena and becomes a council of war, proclaiming its steadfast opposition to some outside enemy. BUCK has a philosophy—individual initiative and enterprise—about which he can sermonize in public. So does SAINT, when there are signs of internal dissension, or even in the face of external threats—on these occasions he can counsel moderation and even put himself forward as a mediator.

This statement of connections between mask and arena is crude, and the example of Bert makes it clear that there is a very large element of 'other things being equal'. Some complications will be discussed later, but even in this crude form the connections can, at least in straightforward cases, be empirically verified. To know that they are true, witness only one instance of the discomfort which is manifested when the mask of STROKE goes to work on a public occasion, or watch the mounting impatience with which sermonizing is greeted in a small action-oriented committee.

There is one other complication. The analysis has been kept simple by treating the mask as a dependent variable: given the committee or the arena, one can deduce the selection of masks available. For the most part this is probably true: committees have traditions and there are collective expectations about what should happen in them. Nevertheless, there are also occasions (not always) when the resolute parading of a mask will alter the nature of the committee, or at least affect its behavior. If, by accident of selection, a small committee comes to contain one or more of those political cripples who have but one mask and this is REASON or SERMON, the chances of that committee, even if small in size, continuing to reach and implement decisions are diminished: and it may be transformed into a talking shop, It seems less likely that the process could work in the other direction because public committees tend to be too large and too likely to contain one-masked versions of REASON and SERMON to permit transformation into a group which furthers implementation by an unprincipled discussion of the capacities and incapacities of particular persons.

Combining Masks

There are people, who, in presenting themselves and their point of view, have only one mask: either they can preach like SERMON or throw out their chests like BARON, or calculate out loud like BUCK, and wherever they are and whatever is the issue, that is what they do. One would expect that, other things being equal, such people would be effective in the appropriate context, and without influence in other contexts. Over the whole scene they are not formidable competitors, yet—this is curious—their presence in a meeting will make other members uneasy.

The reason for ineffectiveness is simple. They have only one weapon, and only one way of using it, and any sensible rival can anticipate what they will do next and parry the blow, or, if sufficiently adroit, cause the one-masked man to inflict an injury to himself. I recall with pleasure the spectacle provided by a BARON, attempting on a public occasion to make the quite legitimate point that the humanities, especially subjects like anthropology and philosophy and history, just because the questions with which they deal do not permit any clear cut right and wrong answers, require a more sophisticated teacher than when the task is to impart mechanical routines at elementary levels in the natural sciences. In obedience to the collegiate ethic, he was trying to avoid presenting himself as a protagonist for his own discipline (one of the humanities) and he evidently wanted not to give offense to his colleagues in the natural sciences. But the habit of combat proved too much and, having put his feet into his mouth several times, each version becoming more offensive as he strove to make it more conciliatory, he was eventually rescued by a colleague in the natural sciences who, like a SAINT with his tongue in his cheek, conceded the point in a few graceful and accurate phrases.

If the one-masked man often turns out to be a booby, and sometimes provides inadvertent comic relief, why should he make his colleagues nervous? If he insists on staying at the wicket when everyone knows that he has been bowled out, he can cause embarrassment and he can delay business; but that is not all. The spectacle which he presents, what he symbolizes, is the creature which cannot adapt. He makes people shiver as they do before grossly deformed persons or monstrous genetic accidents or indeed anything which is blatantly ill-adapted to survival in that environment. Thoughts like this are not in the front of everyone's mind as the one-mask man trips over himself, but at least people hope that such limitations are uncommon among those who set out to direct the organization or the community's affairs.

More effective competitors have a wardrobe containing several masks and some appreciation of how masks must be fitted to context. But the range is not without limits. A chameleon-like virtuosity in slipping from one mask to another tends to be no less unnerving than the one-mask one. Disapproval is phrased in commonsense terms: 'You never know what he is going to do next!' Or 'How could you trust a man like that?' The statement about trust suggests that between the limits of one-mask and many-masks lies a combination which, both in the number of masks and the rate at which they are changed, commands the same moral trust that is given to a person: in other words, one comes again to the four-minute-mile of committee behavior, conveying the message that this is not a mask but the true person.

The first complaint—'You never know what he is going to do next'—encodes a different apprehension. The opponent whose next move cannot be anticipated is dangerous: not only because he may win the contest with that move, but also because he may go outside the rules in order to win and so tempt his competitors to do the same. He is a source of uncertainty because he adapts to his surroundings too quickly. The one-masked man destroys order by refusing to adapt himself to change: the many-masked chameleon changes so fast that no order can exist. He gets written off as 'unstable' or 'without principles'.

The need for consistency—being seen to do predictable and expected things—to some extent controls the range of masks available to a particular actor, at least in public. For example, the man who has acquired the reputation of SAINT will not be a cause for concern if on public occasions he sermonizes about the essential goodness of human beings and their need for one another's love. But one usually seen wearing the mask of BARON, who begins suddenly to preach brotherly love, will be thought either a hypocrite or to have reached a political change of life. If BARON suddenly takes over REASON's line and begins to chop logic, he will be thought to be up to some trick. If REASON one day pushes logic aside and begins to bluster in the manner of BARON, he will be judged hysterical or over-excited, and no one will be intimidated (they might worry about his health). Worse still, if SAINT bangs on the table and lets the raw edge of his temper show, his colleagues will be sad, and pity him, and say that perhaps he has been carrying the burden for too many people too long and it is time he took a holiday.

Between masks which are worn in private one can more readily make substitutions. One reason is that all of them deal with people; BUCK appeals to cupidity, BARON to a capacity to feel fear, SAINT to the need for love, and acceptance as a moral being, and STROKE (and PATRON) will play on anything that comes to hand. The boundaries are not always obvious or high, with the result that the outcome of such manipulations can be uncertain. My claim to be acting as SAINT may be met by your accusation that I am in fact STROKE or even BARON. In public the line between BARON and SAINT is perfectly clear and to play one when the audience has been accustomed to your playing the other, would cause confusion: but in private the signalling can be sufficiently delicate to leave each side uncertain about what mask the other one is wearing. As one would expect, the sharp, clear distinguishing features of front-stage masks are blurred in the unprincipled area of the backstage.

The man who has a reputation for wearing the mask of STROKE in private (it is impossible to employ this mask in public) is relatively free in his range of public masks. If STROKE appears on the front stage as REASON or SERMON, he probably enhances his reputation as a clever unprincipled man. Other STROKES and those many detached cynics who populate academic institutions will, without hesitation, evaluate his behavior as a dramatic performance and say to one another: 'What a clever man! Of course, he doesn't believe a word of it, or if he does, he won't let anything get in the way of doing what he really wants to do'. Those who are naive enough to take the performance seriously will be disappointed because STROKE will go on stroking in private and may have on quite a different mask next time he appears in public. If the man formerly wearing the STROKE mask takes himself seriously in his new role because he has reached his political menopause and, like a *sanyasi*, wants to get himself ready for higher things, he too will be disappointed because people have long memories.

Masks, Time and Theme

In order to carry a mask and attract the attention of the audience while avoiding their derision, one must have the appropriate stature and the right reputation. This reputation may be acquired in two ways: either in action, through a skilled performance, or by a reputation gained off the course. In general, this distinction goes along with that between public and private occasions.

A young university person, who has the required intellectual skills, may relatively quickly get himself the right to wear the mask of REASON or of BUCK. For both he needs verbal and analytical skills, and while these may grow with experience, they do not in themselves require a long period of repeated contact with other people.

The same could be true of SERMON, for this mask depends essentially upon oratorical skill; but in fact it is reserved for elders. Since SERMON deals in first principles, which cannot be defended by rational argument, his effectiveness depends on what people believe to be his stock of accumulated wisdom. The young university person has not had sufficient time to accumulate the wisdom or to harden out the arrogance required for preaching.

By contrast, SAINT, BARON and STROKE are slow developers. They need not be elders, but the reputation comes slowly because it is accumulated through a long series of interactions or transaction with others who spread the word until, one day, the news has gone around to everyone that their colleague is a formidable person or a clever manipulator or graced with saintliness. One or two displays will not do the trick.

The difference is that vividly described in *The Last Hurrah,*[2] between the Tammany Hall politicians supported by a carefully crafted political edifice of 'customized' connections with political debtors, and, on the other hand, the new man-of-the-media, who can make his mass contact by an appeal to ideology and principle. This does not mean that BARON and STROKE, still less SAINT, build their support by means of graft: only that they are required to have a lot of dealings with a lot of people before that support is created. REASON and BUCK can try to acquire their reputation by generalized appeal to ideology and principle. What happened in the novel has not happened in universities. STROKE, BARON, PATRON, and SAINT flourish. The image of a world of personal contacts transcended by new techniques of communication may partly fit the politics of the United States (recent events would suggest that a more subtle combination between public and private activities is required) but it does not fit the university community. SAINT, BARON and especially STROKE, all mainly backstage people, are the ones who keep the wheels spinning: BUCK, REASON and SERMON are paper captains who only make a show of steering the ship.

A reputation which grows slowly is also slowly dispersed. The reputations which enable STROKE and SAINT and BARON to wear those masks rest upon relationships of a community type and in time become to some degree insulated from performance. Just as the person with 'tenure' in a community must transgress not only frequently but also in a spectacular fashion before he is judged to have committed the crime of being 'a bad lot,' so also those who wear masks which pertain to personal relationships rather than to policies enjoy a more long-term, more secure credit. Moreover, they perform before restricted audiences and even when their credit is going down, it will take some time before the word gets around.

It is otherwise with REASON, BUCK, FORMULA and ROCK. Their actions are in the public eye, and they must maintain themselves by the excellence of their performance alone and cannot depend on having friends in the audience who will applaud whether the lines are well spoken or not. One or two bad performances and the reputation is lost, and with it the right to wear that particular mask and still have people listen. SERMON, once again, is likely to be in a more privileged position than the other two public performers. His 'accumulated wisdom' one day will be out of date and will be judged quaint, marking his failure to change with the times and indicating the onset of senility, but, short of this point, the SERMON mask will be taken for granted as a permanent feature in the scenery: like it or not, the Albert Hall stays around.

Finally, the content of certain masks affects their degree of stability and security. This occurs in two ways. Firstly, one way to defeat an opponent is to bankrupt his political credit: to convince others that he does not have the stature to carry his favorite mask. Some masks are more vulnerable than others. SAINT is less open to threat than BARON, for the same reason that more leaders of the Mafia end up in a block of cement at the bottom of a river than do priests in the Roman Catholic Church (at least in this century in this country). In our culture, it is not done to work off open animosity towards a SAINT. The reverse is true of BARON: he needs combat, for without it his mask is incomplete. His motto 'Turn the screw or have it turned on you' tends to make other people very ready to turn the screw on him.

Secondly, in the public arena a man's chances of successfully assuming the mask of SERMON and maintaining it will depend on his preaching being in harmony with some acceptable theme. For example, sermonizing on collegial responsibilities is tolerated *ad nauseam*: so also, on most occasions, is preaching about the ultimate values of scholarship: in contexts where the outside world is relevant, BUCK will find an audience. But the man who chooses, like ROCK, to preach to his colleagues about class conflict between them or about students and junior faculty exploited by the elders of the community, and who is ready to tell his colleagues that they are self-interested hypocrites, will find the level of tolerance low, other than in the restricted circles of those who believe as he does. The reason is obvious: he is drawing public attention to those conflicts and dissensions, which every community, if it is to survive, must pretend do not exist.

To summarize. The pattern is the same as that already identified. The masks which deal with policies and principles and ideologies and the eternal verities (like REASON or SERMON) are to be found on the front stage, and if they are worn backstage they usually cause confusion. Of the rest, those masks which are simplified into dealing with people in just one dimension (they are lovable and loving, or they are fearful—either sense of that word—or they are cost-benefit sensitive) can more readily be worn without embarrassment on the front stage, than the subtler mask of STROKE, just because they are crude and one-dimensional.

The man with just one mask is a political cripple, unable to cope with changing conditions: and the front stage chameleon does not make much impact because he excites mistrust. Both make their colleagues uneasy, because both, in their different ways, invite chaos: the latter directly because nothing stands still, and the former because he stands so still that the world of change overwhelms him. Both portend disorder.

The content of the masks and the fit of sermonizing to dominant themes in the culture will influence the chances of a mask being successfully maintained. It is an obvious point: preaching universal love to revolutionaries or internal revolution to a community of brothers, does not get applause. For a similar reason the insurance premiums paid by SAINT against the chances of being roughed up are less than those demanded from BARON.

Those who can wear several masks will have trouble if they try to combine certain public versions: for instance, BARON does not go along with REASON or with SAINT. But in private, just because there the masks lose their distinctive features and colors, interchange is easier and uncertainty makes possible some delicate political fencing. Successful contestants in this arena are the four-minute-mile men, for the game here is not to hammer simple slogans into the simple-minded, but to create just the right amount of confusion that will let the player win the game without destroying its rules.

The Strategy of the Unexpected

Bert won a victory by sermonizing in a committee in which sermons were taboo, and by wearing the mask of SERMON when the audience was accustomed to seeing him either as BUCK or BARON. In two ways he confounded expectations and yet he won. We should not conclude from this that doing the unexpected will always lead to victory. Why did Bert get away with it on that occasion?

The first answer is because he was Bert. There are three parts to that explanation. Firstly, Bert was part of a community, the members of which were very well aware of him and his history. If this had been a more public occasion and Bert had been unknown, then the few lapidary sentences would not have been enough. The message would have required a longer and more eloquent presentation, for the message alone would have had to carry the day. As it was, since everyone knew Bert, his short statement was carried forward into effectiveness on the back of a known but unspoken, personal history.

Secondly, the content of his statement fitted this personal history. The same sermon, delivered by someone born with a silver spoon in his mouth, could have been dismissed as hypocrisy.

Thirdly, as we noted earlier, Bert discouraged challenge by using the mask of SERMON rather than his more usual pose of BARON. He refused to be combative and so made it more difficult for others to respond in a polemical fashion. Since Bert was known to like a fight and to be formidable, this restraint brought to his side both the community norm of harmony and the 'backstage' norm of being unconcerned with one's own reputation. Both these, particularly the latter, are needed to defuse the detonator effect of a principled statement made before a group of self-styled realists.

Bert got away with it because of his personal history, the concordance of that history with what he said, and his manner of saying it; all drew upon the support of community backstage norms, in spite of the fact that the message itself was an utterance of front-stage principles which also served the interests of a community other than the university.

Another factor in Bert's success was timing. He kept quiet during the first part of the discussion—about whether the admission of formally unqualified people would lower university standards or would inflict an unbearable hardship on those so admitted— though one of these issues was a question of principle which he later addressed. Then he allowed several repetitious harangues on the deprivations which the Ministry could inflict on a recalcitrant university, before he made his move. He spoke up just at the moment when the audience was expecting another set of figures and another materialist argument about what was at stake, at a moment when, one suspects, most of them were ready for a catalyzing statement that would put an end to the discussion and allow them to make up their minds one way or the other.

Leaving aside the question of timing, Bert succeeded because those actions and postures which at first sight appear to be unexpected, in fact are not so at all. They succeed to the extent to which those who witness them, after the first attention-catching sense of surprise, soon come to feel that they understand just what it happening. Something goes on here which resembles the way in which a reader reacts to a novel. In the constructions of novels, as in political contests, there is a fine line between comforting the reader by meeting his expectations and shocking him by confounding them. If every odd page of the novel shatters the expectations which the reader has formed on reading the even page, he soon gives up, concluding that the whole thing is incomprehensible. Every author must, to the right extent, cater to that capacity which we all have as children to hear over and over again the same story and to rejoice in the familiar pattern: the mind, freed from the need to ask what comes next, can feed on the perception of other patterns than mere sequence. But, grown older and more sophisticated, the reader grows less tolerant of obvious sameness, being able, unlike the child, to cope with novelty in a sequence of events. Thus, the novelist who can surprise his reader and, not too often, confound his expectations, is rewarded by attention and appreciation.

But in all this there are two conditions. Firstly, the reader should not be startled too frequently, the penalty being the 'this-is-nonsense' judgement. Furthermore, in the end, all the surprises must be intellectually domesticated by showing the reader that, now he is in possession of all the facts, nothing is really surprising. Novels can demonstrate that the human experience is humiliating, painful, tragic, or ridiculous, but in the end they are rejected if they show that it is entirely without order. Even those who show the hero frustrated at every turn—the Kafka world or *Catch 22*—nevertheless reveal an orderly pattern of frustration. The reader who puts down a novel saying 'it does not add up' is rejecting the novel.

So it is with political strategies, at least in the relatively sophisticated and civilized arenas about which we now are talking. If a contestant makes a move which his rival or the audience do not expect, then certainly he catches their attention. If, on second and third thoughts, the move cannot be made to yield sense, then the mover, depending on the nature of what he has done, is either written off as an idiot or is marked down as a dangerous person against whom precautions must be taken. Bert succeeded because the only really unexpected element in what he did was sermonizing to an audience of realists: in everything else, in restraining his normally aggressive tendencies (SERMON instead of BARON), in capitalizing on his humble origins (without being too obvious about it), and in exploiting his membership of the community (again without being obvious) he did all that was necessary to make the audience feel that this apparent maverick move was in fact part of a larger pattern which any intelligent and sensitive person could perceive. In short, if you intend to do something unexpected, it pays to do it in such a way that the members of the audience can later explain to one another exactly why you did it. The truly unexpected, the truly inexplicable, is something for which most people have no stomach and which, as in the case of the queer rooster, they will eliminate.

This statement holds for 'sophisticated and civilized' arenas.[3] Even in these there are some exceptions. For example, the headmaster, secure in the possession of superior power, can indulge a mildly sadistic tendency by keeping his dependents guessing about his feelings. The more often he carries this off, the more he reinforces his power. If he is challenged, he must risk his superiority by a more direct exercise of power: a direct rebuke acknowledges the fact that power has been challenged, lessens the impression of a game-like interchange and enhances considerations of 'face'. It is a move in the direction of that stockade of unreason with which we began.

The other exception—and it is an important one—to the rule that the unexpected must in the end turn out to be expected, occurred in the case of the prim vice-chancellor who descended suddenly to coarse invective. This could be called the 'dumbfounding' move. Properly done, that is to say properly timed and directed head-on to expectancies, it is very effective, because almost literally it knocks the breath out of an opponent. Because the move is so entirely inappropriate there can be no appropriate response: only a further descent into chaos. But there are obvious limitations. This strategy has a fine point which is blunted by more than seldom use. When you know the blow is coming, you can ride with it and not have the breath knocked out of you. Moreover, and unless your intention is to eliminate the opponent, putting together the pieces and resuming a dialogue in the direction of a reasonable solution is made that much the more difficult. In the context of universities most contests which arise over differences of principles, or even differences of interest, produce truly game-like confrontations which cannot be settled by mayhem, but must be concluded in less expensive ways leaving the players sufficiently intact to take part in a compromise and subsequent cooperation.

Privileged Deviants

Once upon a time there was a meeting (about forty people) of a learned society, a distinguished member of which had died. The death had taken place about a month before, and the chairman's announcement and his suggestion that the meeting pass a resolution expressing its sorrow, was no surprise. Evidently, the cast—or at least the leading parts—had already been chosen, and a senior scholar, a one-time pupil turned opponent of the dead man, rose to his feet and made a speech so replete with all the cliches of sorrow and admiration that the audience began to think of this as an act in rather poor taste, and he might have done better at least to say something about the dead man's habit of—metaphorically—cracking the heads of those who opposed him: he had been a fine polemicist, but there was not a mention of it in the oration. In a small private gathering of people who had known one another throughout their scholarly lives, a somewhat lower degree of hypocrisy might have been in order.

The chairman then invited another man, as it happened, the 'favorite son' of the deceased scholar, to speak. Probably no one thought that what he said was not also in his heart, but his speech was hardly more elevating, for he lacked the talent to express his sorrow with proper dignity and restraint: once again, cliche followed upon cliche, until the meeting appeared to be sinking under a glutinous oozing mound of sentimentality.

The chairman then invited other remarks, perhaps hoping that something more in tune with his own rather brusque and unceremonious personality might emerge, but he was rewarded with two more mawkish offerings to a collective stomach that was already beginning to heave. Then, uninvited, an elderly scholar, best known over the past two decades for his apparent incapacity to think out loud in any way except by free association (his writing was still coherent), rose to speak.

It was, he said, a sad occasion to speak of the death of someone who, like him or not, had left the world of scholarship a more exciting place than he had found it. The phrase 'like him or not' caught people's attention and they began to look forward, with some surprise considering who was the speaker, to words that might more accurately reflect their feelings on this occasion. But they were in for another surprise, and a bigger one. The speaker said that listening to the remarks of his colleagues he was reminded of the Tibetans. To think of Tibetans was to think of birth rituals, and he need not remind his audience of what the Tibetans did with the afterbirth. Evidently he did think that the audience needed a reminder, for he proceeded to give them a vividly colored description of what the Tibetans, so he said, did with the afterbirth, and by the time he finished the collective stomach really was heaving.

That speech was like a detergent or an emetic: the chairman made a clean proposal for a simple expression of sorrow and the meeting passed on to other business, while all but a few of the more solemn members were asking themselves whether the speaker had been his usual inconsequential self or whether he had done it on purpose: no one will ever know.

In a larger gathering of a more public kind, such an intervention might have provoked a rebuke or at least an attempt to restore the funereal solemnity established by the earlier maudlin orators. But this was not done partly because most people welcomed the cleansing of the atmosphere and partly because the speaker, being known to them all, had a license to utter the unexpected: indeed it was expected of him.

Of the many contradictions which one encounters in the study and practice of politics, one of the most difficult to resolve is that which exists on each side of the fine and very unstable line which separates seriousness from a display of humor and irreverence. Every community and every organization, whether or not they write it into a constitution, seems to find a place for someone who does what should not be done and says what should not be said. Certainly it never becomes a free-for-all: who has the license and when he can use it is made quite clear. An obscene insult, traded between joking partners, is merely a joke: between others it provokes a fight. The court jester gets before his time to where Yorick was, if he does not know what things to leave alone. But he can touch some things that others must leave alone. In this respect he resembles the gossiper: he is not responsible for what he says. Those who are not properly licensed for ridicule or who venture beyond the limits allowed them, are no longer jesters but satirists, deemed not well intentioned but destructive, and therefore in more danger.

Some peasant communities allow what the French call '*les jeunes*' to wear this mask of social irresponsibility.[4] Young men between puberty and the time of marriage enjoy the license of extended Carnival, doing all those things which the normal citizen can only entertain in fantasy: perhaps not *all* but at least those which are socially acceptable acts of deviance for young men. They can be prodigal, feckless, ribald, and hell raisers (especially outside their own community) but they cannot go after what the old rooster appeared to be chasing, nor can they be incestuous, nor can they be, at least nowadays, blasphemous.

The license given to these young men, even up to the present day in some places, is a survival of something once more institutionalized. To quote from Milano's *From the Cradle to the Grave*:

These *companies* or societies of *fools*, also called the *madmen*, or the *donkeys* or the stupid ones emerged in Piedmont as a reflection of those festivals of the *fous* or the 'innocent' which were celebrated in nearby France with a strange mixture of sacred and profane. These were genuine expressions of the spirit of association that belonged to the Middle Ages, a relic of pagan traditions, and an instrument of rebellion on the part of the bourgeois against the feudal classes and an expression of the idea of liberty against theocratic and reactionary principles. More than anything else they were satires and parodies of feudal and ecclesiastical organization. Their chiefs were given titles like 'abbot' and they called themselves 'monks', but they were not in the least dressed like monks and carried halberds. They demanded official recognition as the holders of special privileges and rights, like, for example, that of organizing religious and civil festivals, levying taxes on baptisms and marriages, in which they interfered whether they were invited or not.[5]

Eventually most of these associations were suppressed by the authorities for their 'excesses and abuses', and one would suspect that increasing formalization and statement of rights and privileges had begun to remove these 'companies of fools' from the irresponsible world of the jester to the serious world of hard politics: hence the suppression. That is exactly the point: so long as the jester is clearly seen not to be serving (or even more not to be) a rival, he is tolerated because he reminds those in power that there are affairs which never appear openly on the agenda but which nevertheless, must be taken into account. The *donkeys* were responsible, just as *les jeunes* still are in many places, for organizing festivals, not those solemn parts attended to by church and civic dignitaries, but the frivolities which come later—the fireworks and the dancing and the music and the games. Those who are elders and those who are important cannot attend to such things without risking a loss of dignity: but the young have no dignity to lose. Secondly, the *donkeys* seem to have taken on the task of punishing those who behave badly, but who, for one reason or another, cannot be formally reprimanded. Sometimes the offender is too high and mighty to be brought to book: so the *donkeys* make fun of him. Sometimes the offense has gone not against any law or regulation but against public taste: so the young man who married an old widow or the old widower who took a young woman to his bed had to endure a noisily obscene demonstration outside the house on the wedding night. Again, those offenses which are known, but which for one reason or another are not formally countenanced, fall within the 'jurisdiction' of the *donkeys*: the adulterer is mocked and the man with horns is heaped with other indignities.[6]

Finally, in peasant villages the *donkeys* manned those parts of the frontier between communities which lay beyond the reach or beneath the regard of official persons. The Lord or King would not allow his subjects to go to war with one another. They could—and often did—battle through the law courts or through palace intrigues, but the task of maintaining the community's reputation for manliness lay with the young. They could, and sometimes still do, go off to festivals in another community and get themselves embroiled in fights with local lads. As one would expect they were sensitive about the possession of their own women, and the successful suitor from another village had to buy his way through a succession of barriers before he could get to his wedding. Those are the kind of issues that were of concern to the young: the payment of tolls, the shifting of land boundaries, the disputed exploitation of a mountain pasture or a tract of forest land were the concern of their elders, although young men from time to time might be enlisted to break a few heads, if that seemed a useful thing to do.

The activities of the jester and of the companies of fools exhibits that same delicate ambiguity which emerges continually on the stage of politics. On the one hand they are, above all, public activities, self-advertising, demanding attention, speaking loudly and clearly, and they fail if they cannot make people talk about them. But at the same time, unlike others who perform in public, they are not required to take responsibility for what they do and say: in that way they resemble gossipers. The 'obvious' reason why they are not held accountable for their actions is that these actions are themselves of no importance: they are designed just to amuse and to entertain.

But the jester's mask is subtle and ambiguous, because it also makes a serious social comment. This comment makes use of the same kinds of highly personal information that is transmitted through gossip channels, and the jester and the companies of fools punish just the same kinds of misconduct that also are condemned in gossip: greediness, lechery, pomposity, and self-importance, over-indulgence in sentimentality or any other emotion, failure to see things in proportion, in short any anti-social action that is not within the reach of the law. Jesters and the companies of fools occupy the front of the political stage, but their real discourse is addressed to those who live behind the scenes getting things done.

Such people are 'privileged deviants' but if they go too far the privilege can be withdrawn. Once again we come to a fine line of distinction, easy enough to describe, perhaps easy to recognize in particular cases, but very difficult to identify in a general way. This is a line, already noticed, between the jester and the satirist. It is this line which the companies of fools cross at the point when the authorities decide to suppress them. Any sensible ruler will see that the *donkeys* are of use to him: not merely does the steam of resentment become dissipated in their horseplay, but the ruler is given a mirror in which to see his own shortcomings without thereby feeling threatened; people misbehaving are corrected; and in relations between communities the activities of the young permit the community to assert itself in such a way that the rulers need not get their hands dirty. From every point of view, so far, the jokers and the *donkeys* are forces working for conservatism: they are bringing people back into line and they are not charting new lines. The jester is no more than a mildly rebellious figure. He cannot use the same mask to promote a revolution. If he does, he loses his privileges and his immunity. This is what happened to the company of students during the past decade.

In continental Europe and in a somewhat less formal way in the older universities of England and in the United States, students were privileged to do stupid things on particular occasions. In Oxford students cut loose in various stylized ways, after inter-university sporting events (especially the boat race) and on certain occasions for revelry, like Guy Fawkes night. There was also a folklore of inter-college practical joking and occasional fighting: and an equally rich one of what can be done to take the mighty down a peg. But at that time the nearest they came to serious comment on the state of the nation or the university was in the Oxford union debate, and even there, form and style counted way ahead of content. There were no processions or agitations to change the examination system, to change the scale of fees, to introduce new subjects into the university, or anything of that kind. When such agitations did begin, no one confused the new deviance with such traditional forms of rebellion as stealing policemen's helmets or painting lavatory seats with slow drying clear varnish.

In short, although the privileged deviant, especially in the form of a court jester must deploy his words with immense tactical skill around the line which divides the joke from the serious comment, he has few if any possibilities to introduce change. He can restore a situation but he cannot create a new one.

Innovation

So far we have the example of Bert who did something unexpected and got away with it, because his audience, on reflection, understood why he had done it and so were able to remove it from the category of the unexpected. Then we looked at those who are privileged to go outside the rules, and came to the conclusion that this is not what it seems, for there is in fact a rule about how to break other rules. What this means is that other people will accept something new, without fear and without girding themselves up for a fight, to the extent that they are able to work out that what is apparently new is in fact a modification which will bring existing practice better into line with some long-held principle. It follows from this that the politician introducing a measure which is genuinely an innovation must pretend that it is not so: otherwise he has a fight on his hands.

The problem is by no means small. No organization and no community can survive if they are unable to innovate and so adapt themselves to changes in their environment. Along the line between Darwinism and cybernetics, we have come to think of change and adaptation either as a process which takes place without the intervention of a human mind, or, if there is a designer, as the product of rational calculation: the fact that changes are introduced usually in the teeth of someone's opposition often gets forgotten. If you think of any procedural or substantive innovation in a community or an organization, and one that did not slip through as 'what we have always been doing anyway,' you will certainly remember someone standing up and saying 'over my dead body'. I do not mean by this that every institution is equally conservative. The University of London, where I first taught, was an ironbound bureaucracy where at that time it might take ten years to introduce a new course. I once listened to an inaugural lecture in history, which turned out to be a recital of the wounds the speaker suffered on the many days of Crispin when he shed his blood in the committees that eventually came to approve the new degree, which he now professed. Later, I served in another university, a brand new one, where those were judged to have no stomach for a fight who spoke up for what was there the strange idea that new programs should not be introduced until there were resources available to make them work: innovation itself can become a conservative routine. Whichever way round, the point is the same: in practice new ideas and new procedures do not speak for themselves; someone has to fight for them.

This fact that there is usually someone willing to fight to keep things as they are requires comment, for despite bursts of pessimism, the common belief is that of Morgan: men can reason their way out of present difficulties to reach solutions that will make the world a better place in which to live. Certainly some of the opposition must come from those with vested interests, who see their life made worse by innovations which might benefit others. Probably that is the normal source of opposition to new procedures and new values. But, apart from this, we seem to have in our human essence a timidity which makes us think that known procedures, which may be uncomfortable and inefficient but are not disastrous, are to be preferred before new ways which may be an improvement but may equally, since we have never put them to the test, bring disaster. The historian who proposes to work on the port records of Bristol, following in the path charted by those who worked successfully on the records of Liverpool and London, commands a measure of respectability denied—I am thinking of that inaugural lecture two decades ago—to someone whose field is the history of Indonesia. Various technical defences can be mounted for this position—the records are unavailable and are not complete—but in the end such a stifling of curiosity is indefensible by any standards of scholarly inquiry. Nevertheless, it is in fact defended, and often effectively, because the normal person prefers not to take a risk if he can avoid it: least of all does he like having risk forced upon him. In short, in dealing with innovation, we have moved again into that world of unreason in which the heart rules over the head. The farmer, appalled at the monstrous apparition of a homosexual rooster does not stop to find out whether the rooser has really gone queer, or to ask why his inclinations have changed, or what can be done to cure him: he shoots on sight.

The horse of innovation runs with a heavy handicap. Even if it wins, the followers of racing form are going to look for reasons other than its intrinsic abilities, for they are unwilling to give up their conviction that it should not have won. The man who goes off to study the port records in a new place cannot lose provided he does a competent job. But the other historian who ventures into an entirely new field has trouble convincing others that he has succeeded, if only because it is hard to find a standard against which to measure his achievement. The folklore about those who venture into the no-man's-land between disciplines illustrates this. The scholar who professes that discipline quaintly called at Oxford, some years ago, 'mental philosophy' is likely to be judged in the following way. The philosophers will say that he is really a psychologist but it is good to see someone of that discipline so widely read in philosophy. On the other hand the psychologists, acknowledging that he dabbles in a quite interesting way in their discipline, will say that his reputation, of course, rests mainly on his contributions to philosophy. The rate of survival for those who leave the trenches and venture into no-man's land is not high. Nor is the effort to achieve respectability assisted by those adroit people who manage to profit from such a situation: people who in fact are masters of no discipline at all and manage to postpone indefinitely the day of judgement by proclaiming that they are the victims of malice and prejudice.

What, then, are likely to be the effective strategies for innovation, assuming that the innovator is unable to pass it off as 'something we have always been doing anyway'?

The effective decisions, especially those which bend or erode established principles and adjust them to a changing environment, are taken behind the scenes. It follows that unless the innovator has the capacity and the contacts to negotiate successfully in this arena, he will not succeed. Behind the scenes he can exploit whatever personal effectiveness he has and he can make the hard realistic argument for whatever he proposes on the grounds of expediency. He can show that both his opponents and their principles will be diminished if they refuse to bend to the demands of a real world. He does not have to argue for the essential justice of what he proposes—for that may well be something which can be only asserted and cannot be rationally argued to those who think otherwise—but only for its expediency. One suspects that many new programs in teaching and research have been introduced in this way: they will cost nothing; refusal to adopt them will bring severe penalties; the sponsor is going to make himself unpleasant to everyone concerned, if he does not get his way; and so forth.

But the victor is left in a very insecure position. His program has been accepted as a matter of expediency, but not as a matter of principle. It therefore is denied that halo of nonrational acceptance, that unthinking and unquestioning faith which could provide a protective inertia against the forces of revision, that same inertia which in the first place stood in the way of innovation.

It follows from this that acceptance behind the scenes is only the first step. To achieve security, to achieve 'tenure' so to speak, the new program must be made acceptable in the public arena and taken into the security of one of those principled stockades. In short, an innovation is accepted when it becomes part of the sacred. This can rarely, if ever, be done without a contest.

The Man in the Middle

People or objects or events which will not fit into a known category are likely to be regarded with fear, with contempt, or even with loathing: they are not likely to be overlooked. This quality of catching attention makes the unexpected action strategically advantageous: but it can also be perilous. Furthermore, the quality of being unexpected shades into another quality, that of being abominable.[7] Thus, it is not marginality alone which renders the half-breed or the transvestite or the calf with two heads monstrous: rather it is the fact that each culture picks out certain categories of the unexpected, and marks them as *intrinsically* beyond comprehension: they are 'unnatural'. Anyone who attempts to understand or explain these unexpected combinations, let alone anyone who displays them, is likely to arouse immediate and unreasoning hostility. What happened to the rooster, still happens everyday in the correspondence columns of newspapers to those who write or speak in defence of homosexuality.

The chairmanship of a department falls sometimes into this category of 'instantly recognized evil', and the incumbents only save themselves by working strenuously behind the scenes to prove their own 'normality'.

Not all chairmen are in this dangerously ambiguous position. In bygone days, *the* Professor in the universities of the European continent, in London University and in provincial universities like that immortalized in *Lucky Jim*, was expected to be the boss and his subjects were expected to do what he wanted, whether they liked it or not. At the other extreme, at universities like Oxford and Cambridge and in some of the newer British universities, the chairman's power to act on his own responsibility was much diminished by the resources and loyalties which colleges commanded, and in some places there were in fact no departments and no departmental chairmen. In fact, of course, disciplinary interests are so well defined by tradition in the academic world, that in universities where no formal departments existed, necessity brought into being a very active departmental existence, but entirely behind the scene: as one might anticipate, such a state of affairs created, as in the case of Huguenots in Catholic France or Catholics in Northern Ireland a sense of exclusion and deprivation and a consequent lack of scruple and restraint in pursuing disciplinary interests.

The more interesting situation is that which comes in between these two extremes: the chairman who is appointed or elected for a limited period, usually three or five years. The authoritarian chairman, or even the 'underground' chairman, is likely to look upon his own role as an opportunity to build himself an empire: the rotating chairmanship more often seems to be a chore. The latter are the people to whom I refer, in what follows, by the title 'chairman'.

The sources of the ambiguity and the marginal status are clear, and such roles have been the subject of a classic discussion in social anthropology: this is the pincer in which the 'headman in British Central Africa' was caught.[8] Beneath him are his fellow tribesmen, who are his dependents and some of them his kin, who expect to receive his largesse and to pay him tribute, and above all to be treated as persons. Community norms prevail. Above him is the colonial bureaucracy which demands that he should follow bureaucratic rules, that he should treat those in his charge according to impersonal norms, and that he should put the interests of the whole organization before the interests of his subjects. If he deals with his kinsmen and his subjects as they expect, then his bureaucratic superiors will consider his action corrupt and will punish him. If he follows bureaucratic norms, his subjects will withold their cooperation and respect, and accuse him of serving his own interests rather than looking to theirs. Success in such a position is not achieved without subtlety: indeed, it calls for duplicity.

The departmental chairman[9] (and certain other academic administrators as well) encounter exactly these difficulties. When he looks downwards to his departmental colleagues, the chairman's judgements concern quality: the quality of their scholarship, their teaching and of them as persons. To make these judgements he is likely to look for qualitative verification, but the demands which come down to him from those above him in the bureaucratic hierarchy call for impersonal objective measurements like numbers of publications, the success of students in examinations, the percentage of students approving a course as against those who disliked it, the number of committees on which a man served, all of it underpinned by the elusive criterion of a cost/benefit ratio. Those above the chairman want to know what they are getting for their money: those below are likely to find such assessments both spurious and immoral. The chairman is caught in the middle.

Secondly, there are many universities in which the chairman is expected to run his department as a participatory democracy. The decisions are supposed to be reached by a vote, or by consensus, and the chairman is expected to follow them. He is expected to consult and if he makes up his own mind in an arbitrary fashion, his colleagues will protest or may refuse to cooperate in implementing his decisions. Very often he is vulnerable because he has risen from the ranks and within a relatively short time can expect to go back again and presumably he hopes to be accepted as a colleague and a friend. On the other hand—and again in varying degrees—the chairman is the lowest rung of management, a member of an authoritarian bureaucracy, allowed to funnel advice and suggestions upwards, but certainly expected to implement the commands which come down to him. If these commands happen not to match the decisions reached democratically within the department, the chairman is in difficulty.

In short, the chairman is going to disappoint some expectations and lives constantly in peril of being judged neither one thing nor the other, neither a bureaucrat nor a colleague, and therefore an abomination. Such a situation is built to induce a nervous breakdown, and it suggests that there must be strategies for blunting the sharp edge of this ambiguity.

The solution which is open to jesters and the *donkeys* is

closed to the chairman. The jester can do what he does because he is judged to be a person without responsibility: he is merely a commentator, and, moreover, his comments are ostensibly on trivial things. The chairman, however, is not an observer and commentator, but rather a man of action, who has to take the responsibility for what he does. Even if he seeks to be one of those 'custodial' chairmen who avoid innovation, he will be required constantly to make adjustments to changing circumstances. He may cover his actions and his decisions with humor and pathos and even appear to behave like a jester, but if he goes too far and is taken seriously in that role, he can no longer sustain the chairmanship. Both his colleagues and his bureaucratic masters need to accept him as a *responsible* person.

In certain circumstances the chairman can resolve the ambiguity by selling out the position to one side or the other. If his department is unusually distinguished among other departments in the university, then he is in a better position to follow the consensual decisions of his colleagues and, if necessary, to defy the bureaucrats. The distinction of his colleagues gives the department a resource which makes it less dependent on the goodwill of the administrator, because that resource is not under administrative control. At the other extreme, the chairman can go whole-heartedly along with the administrators, ignoring what his colleagues want and merely telling them what they should do: he seeks to occupy a position like '*the* Professor'. Obviously, this is possible only when his colleagues have no resources which are out of his control: when they must depend on him for all which they need. Above all, if he is to do this successfully, he must maintain a monopoly over sources of information coming from the administration: his position is undermined to the extent that any of his colleagues have direct access to administrators. Furthermore, the administration itself must be relatively free from scrutiny and control by personnel committees, privilege and tenure committees, and so forth. Obviously, the man who intends to go back into the ranks in a few years time, will be unlikely to follow this course.

Either of these stratégies will eliminate the element of ambiguity, by placing the chairman firmly into one or the other category: either as part of management or as a colleague.

If the chairman happens not to have the single-mindedness to follow one or the other course, or if circumstances make it impossible for him to do so, and he attempts to steer his way down the middle, what strategies exist to guide him?

In the right circumstances, the position, being that of a broker, can be exploited. Only someone who has never been socialized into the use of mild deceit (and who among them would last long as a chairman?) could resist the temptation to present a caricature of the state of affairs on one side of the barrier in order to manipulate people on the other side. The department could reach a decision and then find the chairman saying, 'They just will not allow it!' Or, he may, like the planner described elsewhere, exploit his superior knowledge of the statistical accounts of resources available (it is a poor chairman who does not attempt to keep his knowledge of such things superior) and argue that, excellent though the program might be, there are no resources available to implement it, or that it can only be done if certain other desirable programs are sacrificed. From the other direction, when resisting orders from his bureaucratic superiors, he may say that his colleagues will simply refuse to implement the plan; or will find ways to sabotage it. Much, of course, depends on the nature of the university and the power in the hands of the administration. But I argue elsewhere the capacity to coerce a large number of people into doing effectively something which is intrinsically difficult to measure, and which they do not want to do, is very limited. If someone teaches four courses well and insists that to increase his contribution to six courses will inevitably lower the quality, his performance is likely to prove him right. Particularly if the chairmanship is regarded as a chore, rather than an opportunity, and if it is difficult to persuade scholars to accept the position, the argument to the administrators 'There is no way I can make them do it' will be effective, and if the administrators are themselves responsible to others above him, they are likely to try to meet the situation by what is called 'constructive book-keeping'.

When a chairman does either of these things, despite the fact that there is an element of caricature and exaggeration in his portrayal of immovable constraints imposed upon him by the other side, his posture is very much that of a man dealing with the real world. In presenting the case he can cajole like STROKE, or show a noble fragility like SAINT or bully like BARON or offer inducements like BUCK, but there is no place for the mask of SERMON or REASON. Most of a chairman's arguments are made in the form of confidential utterances to a relatively private audience.

The chairman, in fact, survives best by keeping to a minimum his public confrontations with others over matter of principle. Certainly in the forum of the Chairman's Meeting he will sound off like the rest of them on matters of principle that happen to take his fancy, but when it comes to managing affairs that could hurt his department and himself if he handles them badly, he is more likely to resort to the tactic of the courtier: going behind the scenes to make sure that the authorities understand what is really at stake in the issue, and, if possible, reaching some kind of compromise with them in private. Thus, in public, he may deliver a tirade about the inequity of exacting six courses from every professor, and the immense cost that will be paid in scholarship and research by running a sweatshop of that kind, but he will, if he is a skilful chairman, also meet with someone in private to find out whether there will be a monitoring system which could uncover 'paper' courses, or whether the administration will be content with 'constructive book-keeping'. The chairman who does not do this, in face of a set of colleagues who sincerely believe that four courses well taught are much better than six courses indifferently taught, is negligent, because he is indolent and prefers the luxury of merely following regulations rather than the relatively hard work of going behind the scenes and finding out what really will be required. There may be occasions on which honesty is exactly what it sounds: there are other occasions on which it is a cloak for apathy and laziness and indifference to the chaos and the suffering that will be the real outcome of a refusal to cope with the real world.

The successful chairman has to be willing to get his hands dirty in the same way in dealing with his own colleagues. If his only contact with them is in formal departmental meetings, where he attempts to browbeat them with regulations and formulae, he will command little respect. The chairman who is not buttressed by the authoritarian status of '*the* Professor', must spend a great deal of his time 'consulting'. He must talk one-to-one with each member of his department, before an important issue is discussed in the meeting, so that he will know beforehand how they are likely to react. This is stroking, the management magic of buttering up all those people who matter in order to make them feel important. If this is done well, he puts a curb on their tendency to gallop after points of principle in the departmental meeting. Just as authoritarian political parties tend to be organized in cells, which cannot communicate directly with one another but only with their leader, so by diligent consulting the successful chairman can inhibit the development within the department of coalitions hostile to himself. The extent to which particular chairmen are consciously manipulative in this fashion must vary. But their survival depends on being able to do so, and this is the message I heard in a statement by one such person who said that dealing 'one-to-one' he trusted people to be cooperative and well-intentioned: dealing with people as groups the only way to succeed was to assume that they were hostile and uncooperative and unable to see where their true interests lay and to drive them rather than to lead them.

The point is this. The contradictions inherent in the chairman's position, his incapacity to meet and satisfy simultaneously the demands of an impersonal bureaucracy and the collegial obligations of departmental leadership, exist only on the frontstage. He can resolve these contradictions by going behind the scenes and dealing, on an entirely personal level, both with the administrators and with his departmental colleagues.

To summarize, the 'unexpected', whether in the form of wearing a mask that at first sight appears inappropriate to its context, or in the form of jesting or in innovations, is of political significance because it catches attention. It makes the audience feel that they are momentarily insecure and their orderly world is about to be upset, and it therefore inclines them towards resistance. The ambiguities of a chairman's position have a similar negative effect. This resistance is overcome if people are able to 'domesticate' the unexpected and the ambiguous by retreating into a world of personal information and personal contact, a world where they can trust the person rather than the idea. Since persons are infinitely more complex than ideas, and require for their understanding an infinitely wide knowledge, much of which is not yet codified, politics remain an art and a gamble, rather than an exact science.

Conclusion

The descriptions and *obiter* analyses of this chapter have been strung along the thread provided by the word 'unexpected'. From individuals choosing and qualifying themselves to wear one or another mask the thread guided us to a discussion of more institutional matters; jesters, innovators, and men-in-the-middle like chairmen of departments.

The unexpected act or event is one which cannot be fitted into a category or a context. To domesticate the act or event completely the audience must be able to identify what kind of thing it is, and then go on to link that class of things with a context or a situation. The actor wins if the audience makes the connections and draws the conclusions which he intended: he loses if they draw an unintended conclusion, including that situation in which they decide that there is no conclusion to be drawn and the act was meaningless.

One set of rules telling the political actor how to wear a mask correctly can be derived from the chart (see page 141). It suggests (many other things being equal—some to be discussed shortly), that BUCKs who stroke or SAINTs who throw rocks or ROCKS who play PATRON would be solecisms or abominations because they make no sense. As a simultaneous combination, such masks deny themselves by internal contradiction: an attempt to combine them within a single repertoire by alternating too quickly between them would also cause confusion. Differences between pairs of masks vary, so that, other things being equal, the more steps needed to connect two masks (the greater the structural distance between them) the more likely will a change from one to the other cause confusion. FORMULA to RATIONAL is a change, but one with much less to be explained away than when a change is between any of the first three masks (STROKE, SAINT and PATRON) and any of the remainder.

A rule like this, however, does not get one very far in explaining what people may do. Certainly, one can see why yesterday's SAINT behaving like a BARON today tends to cause distress, while of yesterday's FORMULA, admitting today the need for interpreting the rules, it will only be said, 'He is more sensible than we thought'. But, beyond these simple cases, the rule remains too far from reality, until other factors are taken into account.

If we adopt the conceptual framework of a structure, systematically linked to its environment, and if we further allow that events which are not under the control of those who manage the structure may take place in the environment, then any changes within that structure cannot be entirely shaped by its own 'grammatical' pattern but even that pattern must in the end bow to the demands of the environment; feedback notwithstanding. It follows that an environmental change between public and private arenas can render acceptable successions of masks otherwise deemed ungrammatical. In effect two grammars are constructed, one for each arena, and there is a pretence that they do not connect. An actor may, without losing points, follow a public performance in one mask with a private performance in a different mask, although if used in the same arena the two masks would be incompatible. For example, BARON in public may become STROKE in private, because the private audience defines itself as distinct from the public audience: they do not carry expectations between arenas.

Now let us turn to the problem of adaptation.

Expectations are relevant. The single-mask man who makes his audience shiver because he symbolizes the incapacity to adapt and therefore the danger of extinction, and his opposite, the chameleon who responds too readily to a changing context (instead of at least some of the time controlling the context), together indicate the most formidable problem in politics. A decision requires not only a judgement on probable outcomes in relation to values but also a judgement on how other people will themselves judge the probability and desirability of these same events. The object of the guesswork, moreover, is a most uncorporeal thing: the trade-off point between the practical discomfort arising from failing to acknowledge a changed situation and the other kind of discomfort which comes from having to acknowledge that what seemed sacred, secure and unchanging, in fact is not so.

The public arena, because the audience is unrestricted and because it is concerned with principles rather than with implementation calls for simple unambiguous masks, and it is at the same time the arena which has the least tolerance for uncertainty and change. (It is primarily within this public arena that the rule connecting mask repertoires with the structural distance of their component masks on the chart could hold.)

Within this public arena there are only two masks which explicitly symbolize change, and only one of these, RATIONAL, is concerned with adaptive change and the relation between a structure and an environment. In comparison, ROCK is simple, proclaiming the virtues of something which is not the present structure, and he is unconcerned with adaptation. One mask, FORMULA, denies the need for adaptive change. The other masks leave the question open.

To get further we need to see the distinction between public and private as a continuum. A list which descends from a senate to planning council to vice-chancellor's cabinet or which goes from university to faculty (of Arts or Sciences or whatever) to department illustrates this. The planning council is private when compared with the senate and public when compared with the cabinet.

Other features vary along the same continuum. Those masks which, like SAINT or STROKE or BARON are acquired slowly, also require some degree of continuing association and interaction between people, a boundary, a restricted audience. By contrast, SERMON, REASON and FORMULA can validate themselves before anyone without first having to become known in the round by a particular set of friends and enemies.

This leads to the proposition that the more a mask requires continued in-the-round contact for its acquisition and performance, the more, by definition, it is played before a restricted audience. But the restricted audience is also a private audience, and a private audience is one which insists less on principle, is more willing to admit compromise and is therefore (at least in this respect) better able to bring about adaptive change. Thus there is a connection between adaptive change and those masks listed under figure 1 in the chart. Finally, let us notice a problem which will be carried forward to the last chapter. The adaptive change agreed upon by compromise in private is neither complete nor secure, until it is adopted on the frontstage and thus given that quality of religious permanence which comes from its enunciation by a SERMON mask or a FORMULA mask.

NOTES

1. See note 8 of chapter 6.
2. *O'Connor*
3. Those patronizing adjectives 'sophisticated and civilized' are intended to exclude despotisms, arenas where virtually all the power is on one side. By contrast, those who need to ask for cooperation and persuade others to follow their designs, must be seen to do things which make sense and not to be acting on caprice.

Wantonly capricious behavior does not meet with approval in university circles partly because it denies the rule of reason. There is in fact quite a rich folklore of capricious acts of tyranny by senior professors dumping upon their juniors, but these are presented as undesirable events and, in any case, the senior person would certainly deny that his act was capricious and would claim that the victim's suffering was amply merited. Acts of tyranny also offend the 'family' norms of a university community.

Even those despots who appear to rule by random acts of violence and terror inflicted on their subjects are nevertheless consistent in their actions. E. V. Walter, analysing the rule of Shaka the Zulu king, speaks of an order which 'can be created by a process that is committed to irrationality, violence, and particularity' (p. 257). Elsewhere (pp. 339–40) he explains that random and unpredictable violence so concentrate peoples' minds on their own chances of survival, that they have no thought left to be devoted to organized dissidence. Such concentrations of power, such absence of any need for political finesse, and such a nakedly instrumental use of human beings is not a characteristic of the arenas discussed in this book.

4. See *Hutson*, 1971 and 1973.

5. This is my translation from p. 90 of the 1925 Italian edition.

6. For a description of these and other customs see *Milano* 104–111.

7. This quality is the subject of *Douglas.*

8. The reference is to *Gluckman*, 1949. See also *Fallers.*

9. The village headmanship and the departmental chairmanship are offices. Despite the suggestion of phrases like 'wearing my chairman's hat . . .' and 'speaking as your colleague rather than your chairman . . .' it would be wrong to think of the chairmanship as a mask. One should preserve the distinctive connotations of 'office', which focus upon the rights and duties of the incumbent. To claim or carry out these, he can use a variety of masks, depending upon the context and the nature of the *alter.* The mask focusses upon the communication and presentational aspects of the job.

CHAPTER EIGHT

Privacy, Community, Order and Change

The Conceptual Framework

Cultural systems are sets of ideas ('myths') about what is desirable and how to extract it from an environment. The systems are fragile. Any set of people who interact with one another regularly are likely to have diverse beliefs (whether about goals, the nature of the environment, or the best ways of matching goals to environment) some of which stand irreconcilably in contradiction with one another. Efforts to impose definitions on each other lead to instability in two senses. Firstly, the distribution of any particular set of ideas may vary from time to time: there are more Big-endians around this year than last year. Secondly, doctrinal struggle may become so total an activity that neither time nor effort are left to cope with the other source of instability: the environment. Big-endians and Little-endians are so busily locked in combat that they forget to feed the hens, and there is an end to it all.

This second source of instability lies in the environment. When one speaks of 'controlling' the environment, the suggestion of mastery in that word is often ironic: one 'controls' heat with a parasol, not by switching off the sun. 'Control' means 'adaptation': adjusting one's own activities so as to produce maximum benefit and minimum harm from forces which are otherwise beyond control. Myths, both beliefs and values, must be changed to fit changes in an environment, which is not under the control of those who assert and argue about the myths.

This is a simple, rational, almost mechanistic way of trying to explain how people take on new and discharge old ideas. Essentially it is REASON's way of understanding the world, and it entirely overlooks the interests which people have vested in their own values. 'Vested' means 'subject to no contingency' and this exactly indicates the tenacity with which beliefs may continue to be held in the teeth of adverse experiences which, at least to other people, clearly indicate that a change of belief would take away some of the hardship.

Why some ideas are intrinsically valued, held on faith and questioned either not at all or only with the greatest reluctance and trepidation, is not at this moment the problem. Our analysis starts from the fact that people behave as if they are unnerved when the foundations of their eternal verities begin to crumble. They resist change and thus, through their religious proclivities, render at least partly ineffective that simple mechanism which is supposed to adjust beliefs to changing circumstances. Our problem, then, at this stage is how to build into the model of adaptive change the fact that men have faith, and that different men have contradictory faiths, in defense of which they are prepared to fight. How are cherished but outmoded ideas discarded and how are conflicts over what ideas should be cherished kept under control?

There is a division of labor, metaphorically speaking, between the different arenas in which political interactions take place. The front (public) arenas deal with matters of faith, asserting and reinforcing, whether in congregation or confrontation, the exclusive hold on truth of the several philosophies. In this arena no serious attempt is made at reconciliation: nor is there any real scrutiny of the effectiveness of the philosophy in dealing with or exploiting an environment. On the contrary, each philosophy is presented as an end in itself, effortlessly superior to others, and beyond accounting because there is no higher goal in the light of which to make an evaluation.

Encounters take place in more private arenas: behavior there exhibits neither the blind support nor the rigid antagonisms of the public arenas. Principles are eroded and traded away, bargains being struck both in the interest of avoiding outright conflict and so as to reach a decision on how to react to a changed environment.

That is an outline of the set of ideas which give shape to this book. Essentially it is the systems framework, with particular attention paid to non-rational behavior. But it should not be thought that I set out to test the applicability of the systems' model, nor even to make the religious gloss upon it provided in Kuhn's thoughts on scientific revolutions or, earlier, in Polanyi's *Personal Knowledge*. The starting question was much simpler: What is the significance of the fact that some political exchanges take place in public and others in private?

I would expect to be able to ask the same questions, linking public and private exchanges with religious (as against rational) behavior—to give it another name—in a variety of other situations, both in universities and other kinds of institution. All that is necessary is the presence of divergent values coupled with the need to cooperate in order to adapt to a changing environment: in all such cases privacy will be the key device. The task of adapting fundamental values to changing circumstances, while at the same time preserving the facade of eternity, is done by segregating political arenas, regulating the distribution of information so that some arenas are public and some are private, and controlling the type of information available in each arena.

This calls for a further examination of the distinction between public and private arenas, to determine what features are best used to discriminate between them when asking questions about adaptation.

Arenas

The types of arena worked out in Chapter 5 will serve to make a beginning: exchanges may take place on the front (F) stage, backstage (B), and under (U) the stage: proclamations of principle, bargaining and gossip. I will stay with the noun 'arena', despite the awkwardness of 'back' and 'under', because that word retains the notion of a performance (as with 'stage') and adds a suggestion of competition.

Each culture has its own 'call-signs' or 'claims' by means of which actors signal to one another which set of arena rules they would like to see applied. A conversation which begins 'Between you and me . . .' or 'You wouldn't believe what I heard about . . .' is clearly an invitation to join in a gossip exchange. An address which opens 'Friends, Romans, countrymen . . .' is evidently intended for anyone who can hear. The call-signs are clear for the public arena and for gossip exchanges, but much less obvious in the back arena. The reason for this will become apparent when we have explored further the connection between privacy and community.

The repertoire of call-signs used in a particular culture to set the degree of privacy for the exchanges which are to follow is a study in itself for anyone interested in political interactions. In this book I have not attempted to look at them systematically, and my focus is rather upon the analytic features which go along with the distinction between public and private exchanges. I now discuss five possible features: the purpose of the actors; the function or consequence of the activity; the type of information used; the degree of responsibility attaching to the actors; and the possiblities for experimentation. The discussion will serve to summarize and to supplement propositions made elsewhere.

Consider first the purpose of the actors. Like everyone else a politician is engaged in getting and spending. He gains support and then commits that support to a course of action.

Among the many forms of support one is derived from being able to shape people's attitudes: to convince them that it is their duty or in their interest to accept as correct some piece of information and the actions which it suggests. If you can be made to agree that the glory of the institution comes from the moral and intellectual training which it imparts to future leaders, then you will more easily drop research efforts and redouble teaching: if you are told privately that X has serious trouble with the bottle, you will be less inclined to vote him into a position of responsibility.

The purpose of the actors both in the F arena and in the U arena is to shape attitudes. In the former they seek support by proclaiming ultimate values and shaping attitudes towards policy and principles. In the U arena attitudes also are being shaped but in this case by passing on private information about persons to get them chosen for or barred from some particular role.

The B arena may also be used for gaining support, as when striking a bargain, but it is distinguished from the other two arenas in that in it support also is committed to action.

The function of each arena is the contribution which it makes to maintaining the system described in the previous section. There is a clear division between F and the other two. F is the place where the various 'basic lies' are paraded, asserted and reinforced through ritual and ceremonial. Through performances in this arena men are persuaded that, despite appearances, life could have an order and need not be without purpose. F is the arena where religion is practiced, where faith is asserted and doubts are suppressed. The doubts, obviously, would concern the resources and constraints which determine how realistic are the goals proclaimed on F. Therefore in addition to the attitude-shaping which serves to proclaim goals (and which will not resolve contradictions between them) there must also be a means of supplying information about the apparatus available to reach the goals and the obstacles standing in the way. Information which concerns persons is provided in the U arena. In the back (B) there is an adjustment both between contradictory goals and between goals and the resources and the constraints of the environment. The statement of function, put in this way, summarizes a main part of our conceptual framework.

The third feature is the kind of information made available in each arena. The relevant distinction, already described, is between information about goals or principles and information about persons. F is exclusively about goals and principles: U is entirely about persons: B is a mix.

The fourth feature is responsibility, the degree to which speakers can be held accountable for what they say and actors for what they do. Being held accountable means that the speaker or the actor loses face or credit or prestige or support or may even be directly punished if what he advocates has consequences which were not foreseen and if these consequences are judged harmful. He also loses if what he claims to be the case is later deemed by others not to be so.

At first sight there seems to be a straightforward progression between U and B and F. A main characteristic of gossip, as our discussion in Chapter 5 made clear, is that information is transmitted under the label of 'entertainment' or 'not for use in action' or even 'Forget that I said it'. Furthermore, one gossips with cronies, whom one trusts, and not with a multitude, so that whether one thinks of numbers or of the specific disclaimers of accountability, it seems that the U arena is one where people are least made to take responsibility for what they do and say. If one then takes off along the dimension of audience, it seems to follow naturally that the restricted participation required in the B arena, and the entire lack of restriction on who may listen characteristic of the F arena must also indicate a deepending responsibility accepted for what is done or said. As you move from private to public, so, if you make a mess, you lose credit with more people.

But in fact it is not so simple, for other factors are involved besides the number of people to whom the information is directly imparted. One important factor is the content of the information. Responsibility requires feedback, consequences and the evaluation of those consequences. If the utterance or the symbolic action is so general that it cannot be connected with any consequence at all, then there is no way in which responsibility can be ascertained. An impassioned speech in favor of 'excellence' may upset those few people who are publicly against anything at all, but until the 'excellence' is translated into more specific terms, there is no way of identifying an outcome and so bestowing praise or blame. In other words responsibility varies with the proximity of the claim to actions and to persons. 'I stand for good government' is a statement so general, so much in accord with the public morality—indeed, so essentially without meaning—that the speaker risks nothing in uttering it to an entirely unrestricted audience. Contrast this with 'Here is my signed order to assassinate the Prime Minister'. Or 'The Prime Minister has had his fingers in the petty cash again.' Both these are specific as to action and person, either have consequences or can be tested for truth or falsity, and leave the speaker accountable.

If the statement or action is specific enough to have consequences or to be testable, then (leaving aside the magnitude of the consequences, the status of person maligned and similar factors which are not relevant at this moment) the original proposition (the larger the audience greater the degree of responsibility) can be maintained. We come back to this topic in our discussion of privacy and community.

The final feature is readiness to experiment, and it clearly is connected with accountability. To say or do something which is both novel and has consequences, by definition means that these consequences cannot be wholly anticipated. The way to avoid personal risk, without entirely closing off the option for seizing credit, is to take the action as far as possible anonymously: if it is successful and can be repeated, the action can then be taken in the open; or, possibly, a claim for credit can be made after the event. We noticed in Chapter 5 that gossip can be made to work in this way.

The F arena, being the place of the 'basic lie', the eternal verities and the sanity-giving pretense of stability, is not the place for experiment, since experiment suggests that present arrangements do not have the excellence claimed for them. Moreover, since this is an arena, it would make no political sense to acknowledge that experiment might improve one's present design for living, in the face of rivals who proclaim its weakness when compared with their own. Lastly even when a novelty is finally validated by acceptance on the front stage, it will always be with the argument that this is not anything really new, but is in accordance with higher principles long accepted, such as the need for excellence.

The back arena is a place of continuing experimentation. Any interpretation of a principle or rule, so as to strike a bargain with contradictory principles, and to allow a plan for implementation and action to be drawn up, is an experiment: a choice between alternatives has been made and the consequences will reveal whether or not this was the correct choice.

These are some features which distinguish the three arenas: purpose, function, information, responsibility and experimentation. One can see many similarities (unlikely as this sounds) between F and U: both are concerned with shaping attitudes, both (each for a different reason) exact a low degree of responsibility and both are remote from logistical and practical considerations. By contrast B is experimental, requires a high degree of responsibility, is action-oriented and processes information which comes to it both from F and from U.

We now turn to a discussion of the boundaries between the three arenas.

Arena Boundaries

The distinction between the three arenas is a fact of ethnography. People may not employ those particular labels, but they make the distinction through the phrases they use and the etiquette they observe in their interactions at meetings. How and why are these boundaries maintained? Are there occasions when it is expedient to cross them?

The circular spy-glass of functionalism reveals that the boundaries are maintained because the consequences of not doing so are disastrous. If there is no boundary to separate off and so bring into existence a back arena, then the contradiction between principles would never get resolved and the resulting doctrinal conflict would bring on anarchy. If there is no reconciliation or compromise between principles, no decisions can be taken to cope with stresses from the environment or to exploit its opportunities. Alternatively, if the front arena is invaded by men of action, there is no discussion about policy, there are no principles to guide action, no religion, no faith and everything dissolves in a flux of doubt and uncertainty. Allow the gossipers up front, you let loose crippling animosities. Pull down any of the boundaries and the result is chaos.

As a statement of consequences, this is probably correct. Remember the consternation when Nixon's backstage tapes (which also had plenty of U matter in them) were shown in the front arena before an unrestricted audience.

But the statement of consequences does not explain why people continue to observe these boundaries, unless the analysis is itself part of the folklore. One doubts that it is. Does anyone refrain from talking before the television cameras about the Prime Minister's fingers in the public till or the Prime Minister's wife in the wrong bed, because he fears he may wreck a functioning social system? Rather he fears for himself and at best, wonders how effective such frankness would be as a political move.

The perils of transgressing a boundary can be stated more generally. Much of what goes on in politics is persuasion. Before anyone can accept a point of view, he must think he understands what it is. In other words, it must be expressed in a language which he understands and which he finds appropriate to that situation. The penalty for using U language (whether in style or content) in the front arena is to be taken not seriously, or to be taken to court for slander, or simply to be told to go away and learn how to behave before coming back. The metaphor of language is quite accurate: it is extremely difficult to manipulate someone in a language which one party does not command.

The result can be no less unfortunate for the perpetrator if the listeners understand the language perfectly well, but refuse to accept it as appropriate. The style blocks the hearers from the content of the message. Alternatively, the listeners may collude with one another to hear something different from what the speaker intends: expressions of personal antagonism are locked off in this way in the front and back arenas (see Chapter 5).

So far the picture is very tidy. There are three arenas, each with its own distinctive style and content of exchanges, each with its own etiquette. It seems that all the aspiring politician need do is correctly identify the arena in which he finds himself and then use the appropriate mode of communication. But this is politics: if the politician follows that rule, he will not get beyond the first steps of the art.

Firstly, he has at least some chance to define the arena in which he happens to find himself. Obviously, it is not the case that everything is up for grabs at every meeting. Only a miraculous performance could turn a meeting of an academic senate into a gossip session. People sometimes attempt the lesser miracle of converting a senate (that variety which is an assembly of all the faculty) into a back arena action-oriented body, and stumble into a wall of boredom and incomprehension, erected by members when served with detail unspiced by argument about high principle.

There are, however, times when actors successfully cross boundaries, and on those occasions (see Chapter 7) the actor takes his audience with him and persuades them that his definition of the appropriate arena is the correct one. Bert did this when he fell to sermonizing: in effect he claimed that the meeting was not about a back arena affair of practical politics, of cost and benefit, but—on that occasion—concerned with a principle—aiding the disadvantaged. He did not blur the boundaries: he shifted the meeting from one arena to another.

There are, indeed, effective ways of mixing arenas, using the style of one and the content of another, particularly when a suitable apparatus for communication is available. The famous Roosevelt 'Fireside Chats' were intended to use the intimacy of conversation with friends to convey abstract and generalized questions of public policy. This is, as I mentioned earlier, the politician's confidence trick and the advantages, in certain circumstances, for those who succeed in conveying the messages of one arena in the style and language of another are discussed in Chapter 7.

Not all shifts from one arena style to another occur because someone, like Bert, has manoeuvered his colleagues in that direction. Sometimes tacitly agreed or spontaneous shifts are made from one mode to another. Meetings firmly established by tradition in one arena, like the senate, seem least open to these moves. But other groups, usually less tied by ritual and etiquette, glide in and out of arenas. For example, the Planning Committee—about twenty strong—tying itself into knots over some complicated but not tremendously important affair, will sometimes drift into gossiping, usually about outsiders who have some slight connection with the matter in hand. Someone asks a question about what resources can be expected from the Governor or the President, because if there were more resources it would not be so very difficult to divide them up fairly. The conversation then shifts into an exchange of anecdotes about the personality of the Governor or the President and of those around him. The meeting wanders happily and comfortably away from the point, losing sight of the need to take action in the warm haze of gossip and mild scandal. Indeed, even if the problem is important but extremely difficult, the meeting may be tempted from time to time to take a 'breather' in the same way. It seems also, at least in this culture, that meetings need a little time to settle themselves into the posture of the back arena. There is usually a period of about five minutes (the time during which late-comers arrive) spent in chatter, gossip, and joking. When the Chairman opens the meeting, both in the formality of asking acceptance for the minutes and in introducing the first item on the agenda, a style is used that is appropriate to a front arena: a statement of the principles involved in whatever is the matter at hand, an assumption that people are agreed on these principles, occasionally tested in a perfunctory fashion by asking whether there is any discussion (and since this is a back arena, there usually is not). Then the meeting, having put principles safely on the shelf, can 'get down to business'.

Meetings which are usually found in the U arena or in the front arena do not show these easy transformations. Compared with them, the back arena is a complex affair, a subtle shifting combination of disparate elements. This is not to say that preaching (F) and gossip (U) are simple things which any unsubtle fool can do successfully: only that in each of these two arenas there is one and only one legitimate activity. Those who wish to do something different can only succeed if they persuade the meeting to redefine itself. Customary front arena meetings (like the Academic Council of Chapter 4) in particular are very resistant to redefinition, not only because of the relatively large number of participants, but also because the meeting's existence as a front arena is likely to have been set by tradition and validated by ritual and ceremonial.

There are firm boundaries, of which the actors are aware, between the three arenas; those who cross the boundary by using an inappropriate style are penalized; and although there are occasions on which successful crossings seem to have been made, in fact this is a redefinition of the meeting rather than a blurring of the boundary. Moreover, although particular meetings (mainly those characteristic of the back arena) may shift from one arena to another, the boundary lines remain intact, because orderly communication and exchanges depend upon a tacit agreement about the appropriate arena. If the period of claim and counter-claim about whether the meeting is to be conducted in the style of a front arena or a back arena continues, the consequence is that nothing gets done because the meeting has impaled itself upon points of procedure.

Privacy and Community

In writings by (and about) university administrators, the term 'community' invokes disdain, amusement or plain disbelief. Clark Kerr, identifying collegial feelings in 'a common grievance over parking'[1] compared the government of 'the modern multiversity' to the United Nations.

> There are several 'nations' of students, of faculty, of alumni, of trustees, of public groups. Each has its territory, its jurisdiction, its form of government. Each can declare war on the others; some have the power of veto. Each can settle its own problems by a majority vote, but altogether they form no single constituency. It is a pluralistic society with multiple cultures. Coexistence is more likely than unity . . .[2]

To the president of a 'multiversity' that is, no doubt, how the world appears. From inside it does not look quite the same. These are, of course, myths, and there is no reason to expect the view from the top of the mountain to be the same as that looking upwards from the valley floor.

'A common grievance over parking' or, as someone else put it (Hutchins, appropriately in Chicago) 'a common concern for the heating plant' contains an undeservedly cynical judgment that academics have nothing in common but a liking for creature comfort. The quip ignores what seems to me to be a fact of experience: a mutual recognition of likeness and a strong sense of being different in kind from those who follow other occupations. But even if I am entirely wrong in this and all the claims of my colleagues and our ancestors were made with complete insincerity, nevertheless, these claims themselves cannot be written off (at least not by someone interested in politics) because they are a potent theme used to guide or justify action. Examples, have appeared throughout the book, especially in Chapter 2 and Chapter 3.

Used in this way, as a fundamental principle in F arenas, the word 'community' carries connotations of amity and mutual concern and respect: treating one's fellows as moral beings rather than as instruments. But the term is also used to refer to collections of people as in the phrase 'village community'. Any study of a community, or indeed even a casual acquaintance with one, shows quite clearly that while amity is the ideal, the practice is quite otherwise: communities are frequently rent with quarrels and faction fights, sometimes even to the point of self-destruction. Universities, too, fail to live up to the ideal of amity. Therefore, Kerr and others conclude, they are not to be called communities. Let me summarize the reasons why I think this conclusion inappropriate.

Three features of university life allow us to use the word 'community'. One is that sense of likeness with other members of the community and difference from outsiders, empirically present and not to be ignored.

Secondly we have some material interest in common. The fact that departments dispute with one another over distribution of resources, that students quarrel with faculty, that alumni have interests which the Young Turks on the faculty do not, does not make this statement incorrect. There is a process of fission and fusion through which those who are rivals in one context will join together against an outsider. A community, in other words, can be viewed as a relative thing: a community in one context in another becomes an arena of disputing factions. I do not mean that the simple fission and fusion model, beloved by the Africanists a generation ago, invariably reflects what happens: actual politics are much more complex than that, the renegade, for example, shattering the neat nesting pattern required by fission and fusion: brother joins cousin to fight against brother. Nevertheless, as a simplified description of how people think the university should work, and how it sometimes does, the nesting pattern provided by individual scholars, departments, faculties (science, humanities, social science), the campus and the university provide a reasonable base upon and within which to build the complexities of political interactions. All the diversity and the discord, nicely described by Kerr, take place within a set of people who normally recognize that they have more in common with each other than they do with outsiders.

There is another way of making these familiar anthropological points, and it recognizes a university as a community of culture. All the divisions—students, faculty, alumni, trustees, secretarial staff, administrators, and the rest—are like tribes; each tribe has a name and a territory, settles its own affairs, goes to war with the others, has a distinct language or at least a distinct dialect and a variety of symbolic ways of demonstrating its apartness from others. Nevertheless the whole set of tribes possess a common culture: their ways of construing the world and the people who live in it are sufficiently similar for them to be able to understand, more or less, each other's culture and even, when necessary, to communicate with members of other tribes.[3] Universities possess a single culture which directs interactions between the many distinct and often mutually hostile groups. Much of this culture can be summarized in that word community.

The salient features of community behavior have been mentioned several times. Let me summarize them here and then make the connection between these features and the arenas. A community exists by virtue of drawing a boundary and excluding some people. Those who live within the boundary develop personal rivalries and particular alliances and have a general sense of camaraderie enclosing both friends and enemies within the community. Community members also are likely to have a basic consensus about fundamental values, which they may express and reinforce in symbols and ceremonial behavior, and about which they seldom debate. Indeed, the values may be so much wrapped up in symbols that members are unable to articulate them in any other way, certainly not in a way that would permit doubt and questioning.

These are also the characteristics which committees operating in the back arena may develop. The evidence has been provided elsewhere, especially in Chapter 4. A number of people who meet regularly as a committee certainly find a sense of their own distinctiveness and in time will come to trust outsiders less, because outsiders do not share the knowledge and expertise of the committee members. Other features will emerge at the same time. One is a consensus on the main policy issues, arrived at through long experience of mutual give and take. They come to a point where they no longer need to argue about fundamental values. Thus there emerges a sense of homogeneity, which goes along with increasing pressure for the members to separate themselves from the outside, both to drop whatever marks of external high status each might have, and to diminish, if they can do it, the degree to which they are individually accountable to outsiders. Their regard for one another increases while their concern for those people whose lives they are managing, if not diminished, will certainly take on a paternalistic style, in which the well-being of the ruled is defined not by them but by the rulers. Whatever the members say, accountability, in the sense of public reckoning followed by rewards and punishments, is diminished.

Remember that we are talking now not about communities, but about the way in which back arena committees and councils may take on community-like characteristics: a concern with persons rather than with rules, a desire for privacy, a tacit agreement not to get into quarrels about fundamental values. The paradox in such a development is that the committees and councils of the back arena are those which in the end carry the greatest responsibility, in that what they do will have consequences; in particular they are responsible for seeing that their institution gets the best possible deal out of the environment. It is in this back arena that the process of keeping myths not too far out of touch with reality goes on. But the very process of translating ideas into action, building that community-like thorn hedge around the committee, tends to diminish members' own perception of the reality around them. The feedback from what they do for the most part falls on those outside the committee or the council, and the more they develop the characteristics needed to operate in the backstage arena the less they are willing to consult. The less they consult, the more slowly do they hear about emergencies arising from changes in the outside world.

The reality-testing device in our conceptual framework, the committee which defines itself as working in a back arena, seems then to be (like eyes) subject to cataracts, which, as they grow, impair the capacity to perceive what must be done. In the final section, on myth and reality, we look at analogies of ways to prevent blindness.

Myth and Reality

The problem is that committees and councils in the back arena take on community-like characteristics. The disregard for principles, which makes them able to deal with the strains and stresses coming from the environment, the pressures of having to cope with difficulties, the need to take action, and the growing perception that they have special skills which the rest of the population do not and which must be exercised in the interest of that population, encourage an elite mentality and a paternalistic outlook, which in the end make them willing to listen more to themselves and less to the voices of those on whose behalf they are acting. They lose sensitivity and they lose their ability to stay in touch with reality.

Many institutions have evolved mechanical devices for dealing with this problem. Generally it is recognized not so much as a lack of sensitivity in perceiving problems, but rather as a growing self-centredness, an increasing tendency to serve their own interests rather than the interests of the larger population for whom the group is supposed to be acting. In other words, people become corrupt. Thus there are rules about rotation. Members may serve on committees of this kind only for a limited period. Civil servants in India were transferred from district to district at regular intervals to prevent them from diluting the pure impersonal standards of bureaucracy with the warmth of friendship and favoritism. If the members are moved on at regular intervals, it becomes that much the more difficult to develop community-like feelings within the committee, and the committee thus remains sensitive to pressures from outside.

A more direct way of bringing about the same end is to choose the committee members by means of elections, which also take place at regular intervals. Thus each member has a constituency, to the members of which he is answerable at the next poll, and in this way his inclination to form alliances with fellow members of a committee or council and forget those outside it is diminished.

A third way of preventing the decline and fall into insensitivity is to build systematic checks and balances between committees or between committee and officials. For example, there is such a check between the Personnel Committee, described in Chapters 4 and 5, and the administrative official, the Vice-Chancellor or President. The latter's tendency to back his favorites is held in check by the knowledge that the Personnel Committee may cause him considerable embarrassment if he does so too openly. From the other direction, because the Chancellor or President takes responsibility for the decision and will feel the hot wind of disfavor if he makes too many inept or unintelligent decisions, he cannot allow his advisors to get too far out of touch with the institution's needs and to become obsessed with maintaining patterns set merely by precedent.

These and other devices are the practical implementations of more deep-seated tendencies.

The people who guide human institutions must find their way between the poles of religion and of science. The scientific end represents systematic doubt and the willingness to learn from experience: the religious end enshrines security and stability and gives the assurance that things will happen in the future as they have happened in the past. The back-arena committees and councils, as they drift towards a community-style of conducting their affairs and an increasing insensitivity to experience, are moving towards the religious end of the continuum. The need to avoid crippling debate about first principles, the desire to avoid an audience and, above all, the necessity for taking action, all push them in this direction. Behind this there seems to be a fundamental tendency in human and cultural affairs towards conservatism.

One hesitates to speak about 'human nature' and I do so without any systematic backing from experiment. Nevertheless, even the small experience of writing this book and having others read it, makes it hard to avoid the conclusion that such a tendency exists. To speak about 'myths' provokes people into asking about the reality behind the myths. To speak about 'masks' suggests a level of unreality and make-believe, behind which exists a real world of real people. One man, who read an earlier version, went out and delivered a lecture to student teachers on the need to present themselves honestly and without pretence, without a mask. The real teacher, gifted with knowledge and grace, had no need for pretence. He was asked whether he was not himself, at that very moment, wearing a mask: not unexpectedly, he chose to treat the question as a low blow. With few exceptions, critics have suggested that the real problem is to find the real person behind the mask. Indeed, the material itself supports this view: the 'four-minute-mile' man in committee behavior is the man who can convince others that he has dropped all masks and is revealing his own true self.

But the evident desire that there should be some underlying, firm and stable reality beneath the flux of appearances is no proof that there is such a reality. It is evidence only that we desire such a reality and that we bend our every effort into setting up procedures that will allow the pretence to seem plausible. So the elite committees, making themselves increasingly insensitive to the real world with which they must find adjustment, are doing no more than indulging the religious tendencies which are the hallmark of the front arenas.

There is even, in some cultures—not least in present-day America—a religious counter to elitist myopia. Confidentiality and privacy are labeled 'secrecy'[4] and branded as absolute evils, at least within the community. Secrecy can be defended only in the face of an external enemy and within the community everyone has a right to know everything. No one dares to defend confidentiality on the grounds that it permits efficient management: the only public defense, whether of the Watergate affair or anything else, is offered under the name of national security.

No institution, no community, no society could survive under such conditions of absolute openness. All decisions would be taken under the guidance of principles, contradictions between principles would be left unmuted and uncompromised, and everything would be a play for an audience rather than an attempt to cope with a brute and complicated reality.[5] Since we survive, and most of us want to survive, campaigns to open everything to public scrutiny in the end do no more than shift out one set of elitist rulers and put another set in their place.

Moreover the desire to have everything open, above-board, and done by the book which everyone can read flies in the face of another human tendency which has been exemplified again and again in these chapters: the wish to be treated as a moral being rather than an instrument in the service of an institution. The fear of secrecy is a manifestation of mistrust: a conviction that others are essentially malevolent, self-interested and incapable of altruism. Certainly we have that feeling in us. But we also have the opposite: a knowledge that as we are willing to work for the benefit of others, so they will work for our benefit. Without trust, there is no society. With trust, 'secrecy' becomes irrelevant: it is replaced by 'confidence', which is, in fact, another word for trust.

So, at the end, we come to the real dilemma which far transcends, while it encompasses, the three-way pull of scholarship, collegiality and service. It is in reality a choice between equal evils: the open world of principle and the shadowed world of action. To choose one or the other is foolish, and the sensible man can only pilot his way between them. In the end it makes no sense to ask who steers the ship: Is it morality or expediency? Are the men in the smoke-filled rooms really those at the helm? They may be at the helm, but if there are no principles and there is no front arena, they have no course by which to steer.

Scylla is the rock of principle: expediency is Charybdis. Politics being what they are, the ship seldom contrives to steer a straight course between them. Usually, if there is progress, it is achieved by bouncing from one rock to another.

NOTES

1. *Kerr*, p. 20.

2. *Kerr*, p. 36.

3. When I wrote this I had in mind some remarks in the introduction to *Leach*. But the use of the term 'community' makes clear that awareness of unity in the apparent diversity of cultures and customs is a part of a model known to the actors and not to the analyst alone.

4. I have in mind not only that fine committed classic *The Torment of Secrecy* by Edward Shils, but also the entertaining confusions caused between the Buckley measures, a well-intentioned boost for privacy which makes it an offense to put up a list of names of students with the marks awarded for an examination, and, on the other hand, various mindless measures designed to make every record and every activity, whether judicial or political, open to the public gaze. (See also the grimly entertaining account in Bunzel).

5. '[Politicians] know how much of the art of politics lies in concealing behind a facade of rigid adherence to immutable principle those deviations and reversals which events and responsibility so often force upon governments' (Blake, p. 764).

References

Bailey, F.G. 1965 'Decisions by Consensus in Councils and Committees' in *Political Systems and the Distribution of Power* Banton, M. (ed.). London: Tavistock.

Bailey, F. G. (ed.) 1971 *Gifts and Poison* Oxford: Blackwell.

Bailey, F. G. 1972 'Tertius Gaudens aut Tertium Numen' Burg Wartenstein Symposium, No. 55.

Bailey, F. G. (ed.) 1973 *Debate and Compromise* Oxford: Blackwell.

Barth, Fredrik 1959 *Political Leadership Among Swat Pathans* London: Athlone Press.

Belshaw, Cyril S. 1974 *Towers Besieged: The Dilemma of the Creative University* Toronto: McClelland and Stewart.

Blake, Robert 1966 *Disraeli* London: Eyre and Spottiswoode (1969 London: Methuen).

Blaxter, Loraine 1971 'Rendre Service and Jalousie' in *Gifts and Poison* Bailey, F. G. (ed.) Oxford: Blackwell.

Brunzel, John 1975 'The Eclipse of Confidentiality' in *Change*.

Burling, Robbins 1964 'Cognition and Componential Analysis: God's Truth or Hocus-Pocus?' in *American Anthropologist* Vol. 66.

Burridge, K. O. L. 1969 *New Heaven New Earth* Oxford: Blackwell.

Cassirer, Ernst 1944 *An Essay on Man* New Haven and London: Yale University Press.

Clark, Burton 1963 'Faculty Culture' in *The Study of Campus Cultures* Lunsford, Terry F. (ed.) Berkeley: Centre for the Study of Higher Education.

Colson, E. 1953 *The Makah Indians* Manchester: Manchester

University Press.

Cornford, F. 1953 *Microcosmographia Academica Being a Guide for the Young Academic Politician* Cambridge: Bowes and Bowes (first published 1908).

Coser, Lewis 1956 *The Functions of Social Conflict* London: Routledge and Kegan Paul.

Devons, E. 1961 'Statistics as a Basis for Policy' in *Essays in Economics* London: George Allen and Unwin.

Douglas, Mary 1966 *Purity and Danger* London: Routledge and Kegan Paul.

Dumount, Louis 1970 'World Renunciation in Indian Religions' in *Religion, Politics and History in India* Paris: Mouton.

Fallers, Lloyd n.d. (c. 1955) *Bantu Bureaucracy* Cambridge: Heffer.

Frake, Charles O. 1964 'Further Discussion of Burling' *American Anthropologist* Vol. 66.

Frankenberg R. 1957 *Village on the Border* London: Cohen and West.

Frankenberg R. 1972 'Taking the blame and passing the buck, or, The carpet of Agamemnon: an essay on the problems of responsibility, legitimation and triviality' in *The Allocation of Authority* Gluckman, M. (ed.) Manchester: Manchester University Press.

Gluckman, M. (with J. C. Mitchell and J. A. Barnes) 1949 'The Village Headman in British Central Africa' in *Africa* XIX.

Gluckman, M. 1963 'Gossip and Scandal' *Current Anthropology* Vol. 4.

Gluckman, M. (ed.) 1972 *The Allocation of Responsibility* Manchester: Manchester University Press.

Hutchins, Robert Maynard 1956 *Freedom, Education and The Fund: Essays and Addresses, 1946-1956* New York: Meridian Books.

Hutson, Susan 1971 'Social Ranking in a French Alpine Community' in *Gifts and Poison* Bailey, F. G. (ed.) Oxford: Blackwell.

Hutson, Susan 1973 'Valloire' in *Debate and Compromise* Bailey, F. G. (ed.) Oxford: Blackwell.

Hymes, Dell H. 1964 'Discussion of Burling's Paper' *American Anthropologist* Vol. 66.

Kerr, Clark 1972 *The Uses of the University* Cambridge: Harvard University Press.

Kuhn, Thomas S. 1970 *The Structure of Scientific Revolutions* Chicago: Chicago University Press (2nd edition, enlarged).

Leach, E. R. 1954 *Political Systems of Highland Burma* London: Bell.

Lunsford, Terry F. 1970 *The Official Perspective in Academe* Berkeley: Centre for Research and Development in Higher Education.

Mair, Lucy 1962 *Primitive Government* Harmondsworth: Penguin.

Malinowski, B. 1948 *Magic, Science and Religion and Other Essays* Glencoe: The Free Press.

Mauss, Marcel 1938 'Une Catégorie de l'Esprit Humain: la Notion de Personne, celle de "Moi". Un Plan de Travail' *Journal of the Royal Anthropological Institute* Vol. LXVIII.

Mayer, Adrian C. 1966 'Quasi-Groups in the Study of Complex Societies' in *The Social Anthropology of Complex Societies* Banton, M. (ed.) London: Tavistock.

Milano, Euclide 1925 *Dalla Culla alla Bara: Usi Natalizi, Nuziali e Funerei nella Provincia di Cuneo*. Borgo S. Dalmazzo: Instituto Grafico Bertello & Comp.

Morgan, Lewis Henry 1962 *League of the Iroquois* New York: Corinth Books (first published as *League of the Ho-De-No-Saunee or Iroquois* Rochester, New York, 1851).

Morgan, Lewis Henry 1868 *The American Beaver and His Works* Philadelphia: Lippincott.

Murray, Gilbert 1912 *Five Stages of Greek Religion* New York: Doubleday (1951 edition).

O'Connor, E. 1959 *The Last Hurrah* London: Pantheon.

O'Toole, Simon 1970 *Confessions of an American Scholar* Minneapolis: University of Minnesota Press.

Parsons, Talcott, Platt, Gerald M. 1973 *The American University* Cambridge: Harvard University Press.

Polanyi, Michael 1958 *Personal Knowledge* Chicago: Chicago University Press.

Pritchett, V. S. 1973 *Balzac* New York: Knopf.

Radcliffe-Brown, A. R. 1940 *Preface to African Political Systems* Evans-Pritchard, E. E., Fortes, M (eds.) London: Oxford University Press.

Resek, Carl 1960 *Lewis Henry Morgan: American Scholar* Chicago: Chicago University Press.

Rudolph, Frederick 1962 *The American College and University: A History* New York: Knopf.

Sahlins, M. D. 1963 'Poor Man, Rich Man, Big Man, Chief: Political Types in Melanesia and Polynesia' *Comparative Studies in Society and History* Vol. 5.

Salingar, L. G. 1955 'The Elizabethan Literary Renaissance' in *The Age of Shakespeare* Ford, Boris (ed.) Harmondsworth: Penguin.

Shils, Edward 1956 *The Torment of Secrecy* Glencoe: The Free Press.

Sorel, Georges 1908 *Reflections on Violence* Hulme, T. E., Roth, J. (trans.) New York: Collier (1970 edition).

Stern, B. J. 1967 *Lewis Henry Morgan: Social Evolutionist* New York: Russell and Russell (first published 1931).

Strauss, Anselm L. 1959 *Mirrors and Masks: the Search for Identity* Glencoe: The Free Press.

van den Berghe, Pierre 1970 *Academic Gamesmanship: How to Make a Ph.D. Pay.* London: Abelard-Schuman.

van Velsen, J. 1969 'Procedural Informality, Reconciliation, and False Comparisons' *Ideas and Procedures in African Customary Law* Gluckman, M. (ed.) London: Oxford University Press.

Veblen, Thorstein, 1954 *The Higher Learning in America* Stanford, California: Academic Reprints.

Walter, E. V. 1969 *Terror and Resistance: A Study of Political Violence* New York: Oxford University Press.

Index